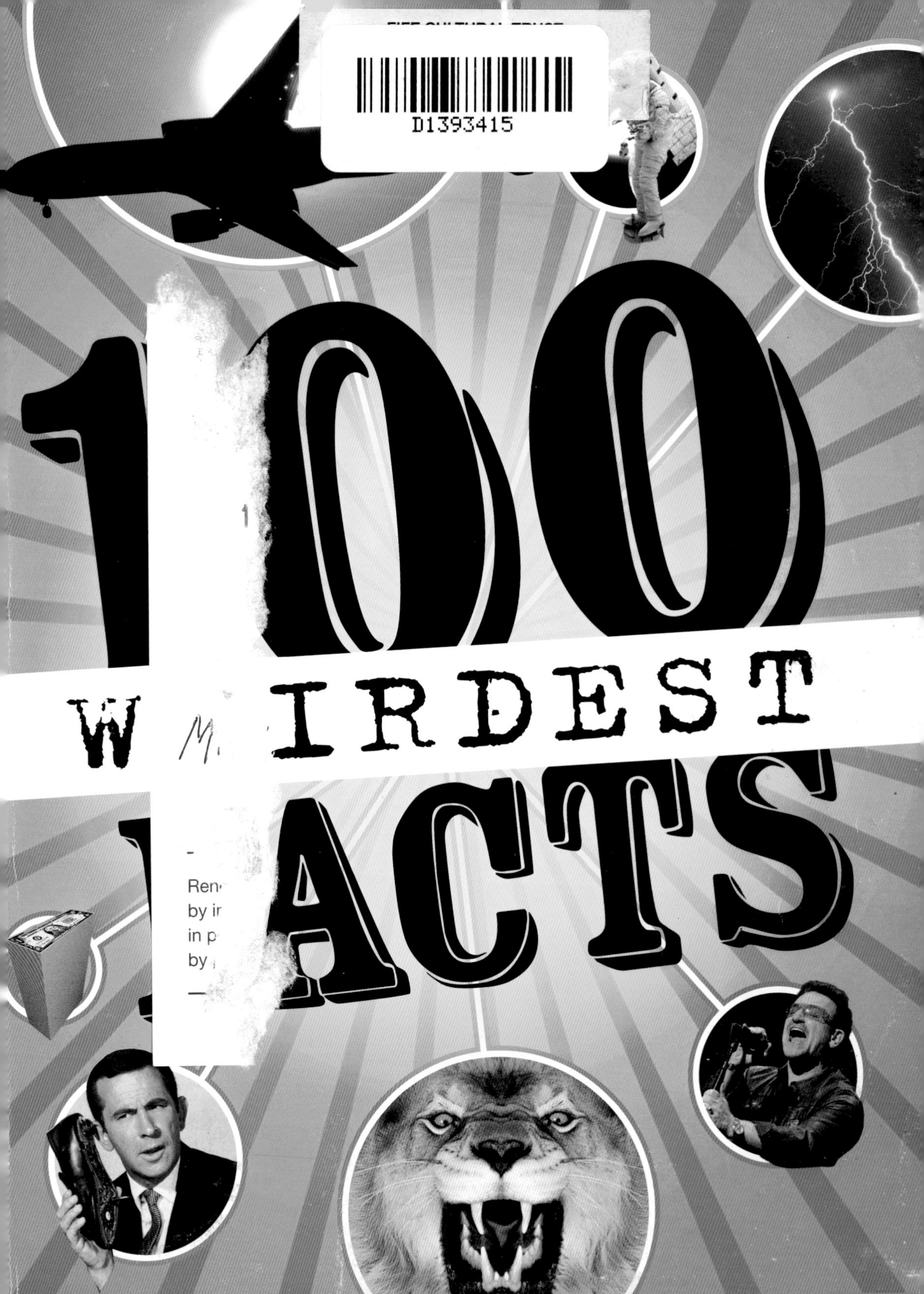
D1393415
IRDEST
ACTS

Editorial and Design: Dynamo Ltd
QED Project Editor: Alexandra Koken

First published by the UK in 2013 by
QED Publishing
A Quarto Group company
230 City Road
London EC1V 2TT

www.qed-publishing.co.uk

A catalogue record for this book is available from the British Library.

ISBN 978 1 78171 085 2

Printed in China

100 WEIRDEST FACTS

QED
QED Publishing

CONTENTS

A cheetah can out sprint most cars.

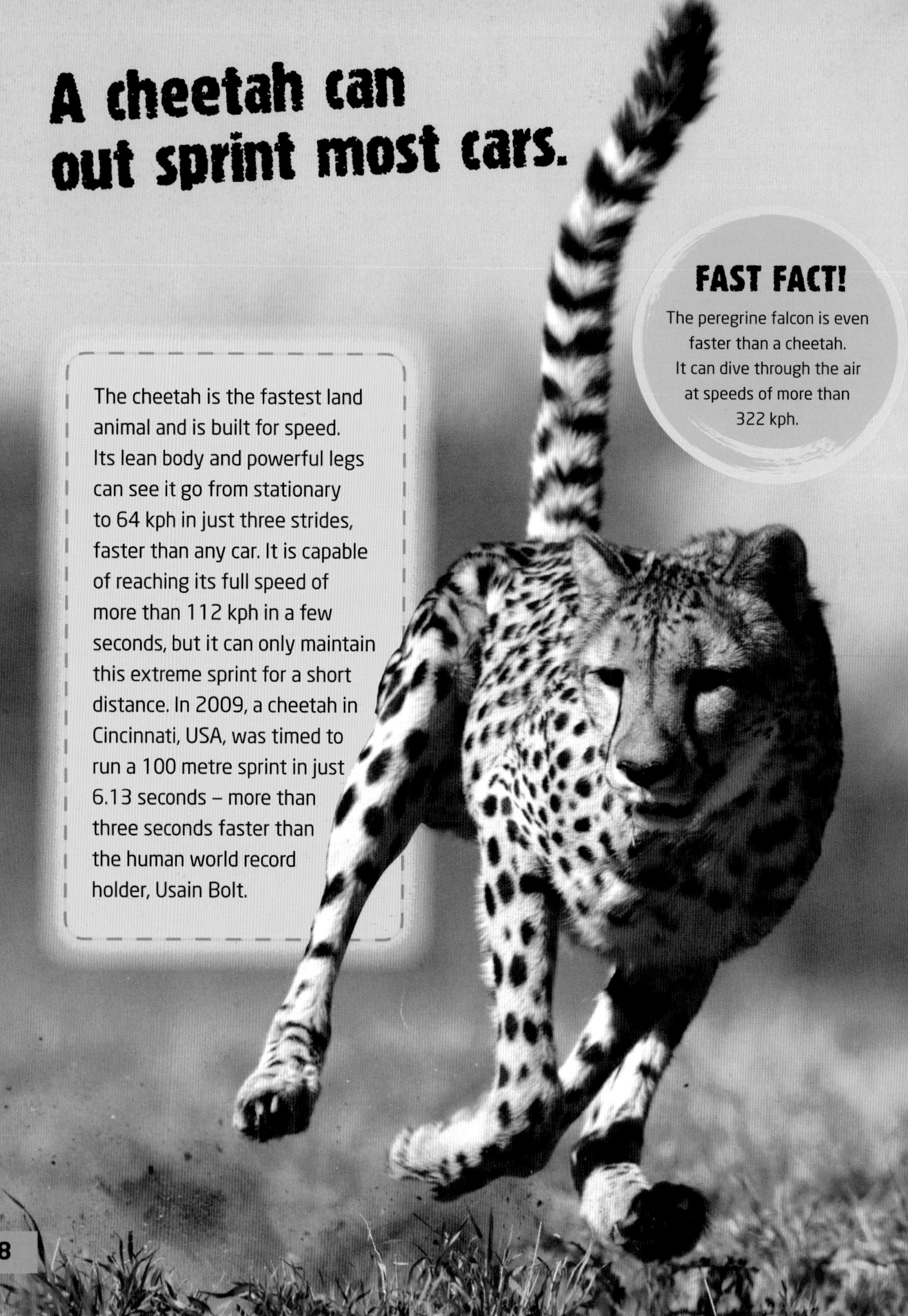

The cheetah is the fastest land animal and is built for speed. Its lean body and powerful legs can see it go from stationary to 64 kph in just three strides, faster than any car. It is capable of reaching its full speed of more than 112 kph in a few seconds, but it can only maintain this extreme sprint for a short distance. In 2009, a cheetah in Cincinnati, USA, was timed to run a 100 metre sprint in just 6.13 seconds – more than three seconds faster than the human world record holder, Usain Bolt.

FAST FACT!

The peregrine falcon is even faster than a cheetah. It can dive through the air at speeds of more than 322 kph.

Some misbehaving Aztec children were beaten with spiny plants.

If you were a naughty child in the time of the Aztec civilization in Central America about 8000 years ago, you had to watch out. One of the punishments historians believe Aztec children faced was a beating with the spiny leaves of the maguey plant (also known as the Agave americana) until they were bleeding.

FAST FACT!

Another cruel Aztec punishment was burning red-hot chilli peppers over a fire and letting the spicy smoke sting the victim's eyes and nostrils.

Giant stones are used as money on one Pacific island.

The small Pacific island of Yap, one of the Caroline Islands, has an unusual currency. Stone discs, carved out of calcite rock, were commonly used to buy goods and services in the past, although today the US dollar is mostly used.

What makes Yap's stone money really interesting is how H-U-G-E some of the stones are. The largest measures 3.6 metres in diameter and needs more than a dozen adults to lift it.

FAST FACT!

The first paper money was used about 1200 years ago in China during the Tang Dynasty.

Nepal is the only country with a flag that isn't rectangular or square.

FAST FACT!

The origin of the word *flag* comes from the Saxon word *fflaken* - meaning to fly or float in the air.

National flags come in all colours and designs. The only square flags are those of Switzerland and the Vatican City, while Mozambique's is the only national flag to feature a firearm, an AK-47 rifle, on its design.

Vatican City flag

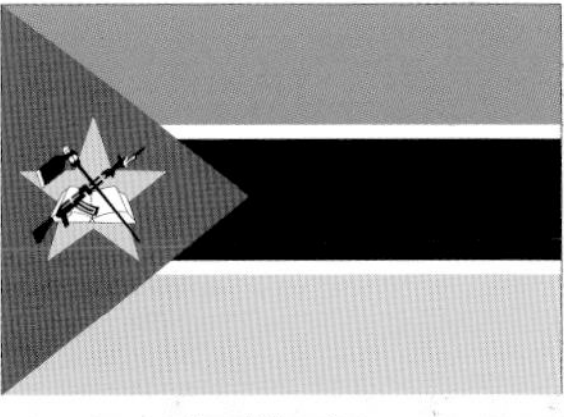

Mozambique flag

The flag of the Asian nation of Nepal was officially introduced in 1962. It has five sides and looks like two triangles stacked on top of each other.

You cannot tickle yourself.

FAST FACT!

Another thing almost everyone on the planet cannot do is lick their elbow. Go on, try it!

Most people are ticklish and have a special spot – perhaps their tummy, their armpits or the backs of their knees – that makes them giggle when it's tickled by someone else. But no matter how hard you try, you cannot tickle yourself.

Scientists think that the answer lies in part of the brain called the cerebellum. This area performs lots of different tasks, such as controlling your balance and movement. It may also help you to ignore and not react to sensations you expect – like when you attempt to tickle yourself.

More than 3 million emails are sent round the world every single second.

FAST FACT!

Despite the boom in emails, there was no morse code for the @ sign until 2004. The morse code for the @ sign is . - - . - . (dot dash dash dot dash dot).

It is believed that the first email was sent by a US computer programmer called Ray Tomlinson in 1971. At the time, it wasn't thought of as a big deal, but as more and more people got computers and had access to the Internet, emails became the perfect way to send messages, photographs or other computer files to people all around the world.

More than 2 billion people have one or more email accounts, and about 280 billion emails are sent every day – more than 3 million per second.

Leonardo da Vinci wrote his notes backwards.

A gifted artist, inventor and thinker, Leonardo da Vinci filled his notebooks with backwards writing, which could only be read using a mirror. There are more than 6000 pages of these notes in existence. Among Da Vinci's amazing achievements were designs for flying machines and tanks, amazing anatomical drawings of the human body and famous paintings such as the *Mona Lisa*.

FAST FACT!

The *Mona Lisa* has been stolen and vandalized on a number of occasions, and it once even went missing for two years. Now it sits safely at the Louvre Museum in Paris, France.

An ice hockey puck struck by Zdeno Chára of the Boston Bruins reached a speed of 175 kph.

FAST FACT!

Some early hockey pucks were made of wood. The first rubber puck was used in a match held in Montreal, Canada, in 1875.

At 2.06 metres tall, the Slovakian defender Zdeno Chára is the tallest player to compete in the National Hockey League (NHL).

In 2009, Chára hit the hardest ever NHL shot of 169.6 kph during the Superskills Competition in Montreal, Canada. Three years later, in Ottawa, he broke his own record with a shot reaching 175 kph, which is the hardest recorded NHL shot today.

Walt Disney banned his staff from growing moustaches for 40 years.

Walt Disney had a moustache himself, but he wanted the staff at his theme parks to convey a clean-cut image. So in the mid-1950s he introduced a staff code that banned beards, long hair and moustaches. Even though Disney died in 1966, the ban on moustaches remained in place and wasn't lifted until 2000. The ban on beards was only removed in 2012.

FAST FACT!

Walt Disney has had more nominations for Oscars than any other person – a staggering 59 in total.

A man was struck by lightning SEVEN different times and survived them all.

Roy Sullivan was 30 years old when he was first struck by lightning in 1942. By 1977, the US park ranger, who worked at Shenandoah National Park in Virginia, had suffered an incredible seven lightning strikes. Some occurred while working in the park, but the last happened while he was out fishing. Most left parts of his body scorched, although the fourth strike in 1972 set his hair on fire. Sullivan's wife was also struck once by lightning, while she was hanging out the washing.

FAST FACT!

Lightning is a sudden discharge of electricity. This can heat up the air to very high temperatures – more than than 22,204 °C.

A man tied 45 helium balloons to a garden chair and ended up flying more than 4570 metres into the air.

In 1982, Larry Walters decided to take off from his garden in San Pedro, California, in the USA. He attached his chair to a bunch of 2.4-metre-wide balloons filled with helium – a gas that's lighter than air – and rose to an altitude of more than 4570 metres. He shot some of the balloons with a pellet gun to descend, but dropped the gun. Eventually, his balloons got tangled up in a power line, causing a 20-minute electricity blackout. Amazingly, he made it safely back down to the ground.

FAST FACT!

Larry Walters always wanted to become a pilot with the United States Air Force, but couldn't because of his poor eyesight.

The shortest ever war lasted less than 45 minutes!

In 1896, British forces went to war against the forces of the Sultan of Zanzibar, an island in the Indian Ocean (now part of Tanzania). Five British ships and land forces were given the order to attack the Sultan's Palace in Zanzibar Town at nine o'clock in the morning, and firing began two minutes later. Before the clocks had reached 9.45 a.m., the war was over. The Sultan fled, and the British installed a new ruler.

FAST FACT!

The Isles of Scilly, off the southwestern coast of England, and the Netherlands were technically at war for over 300 years, but no shots were fired.

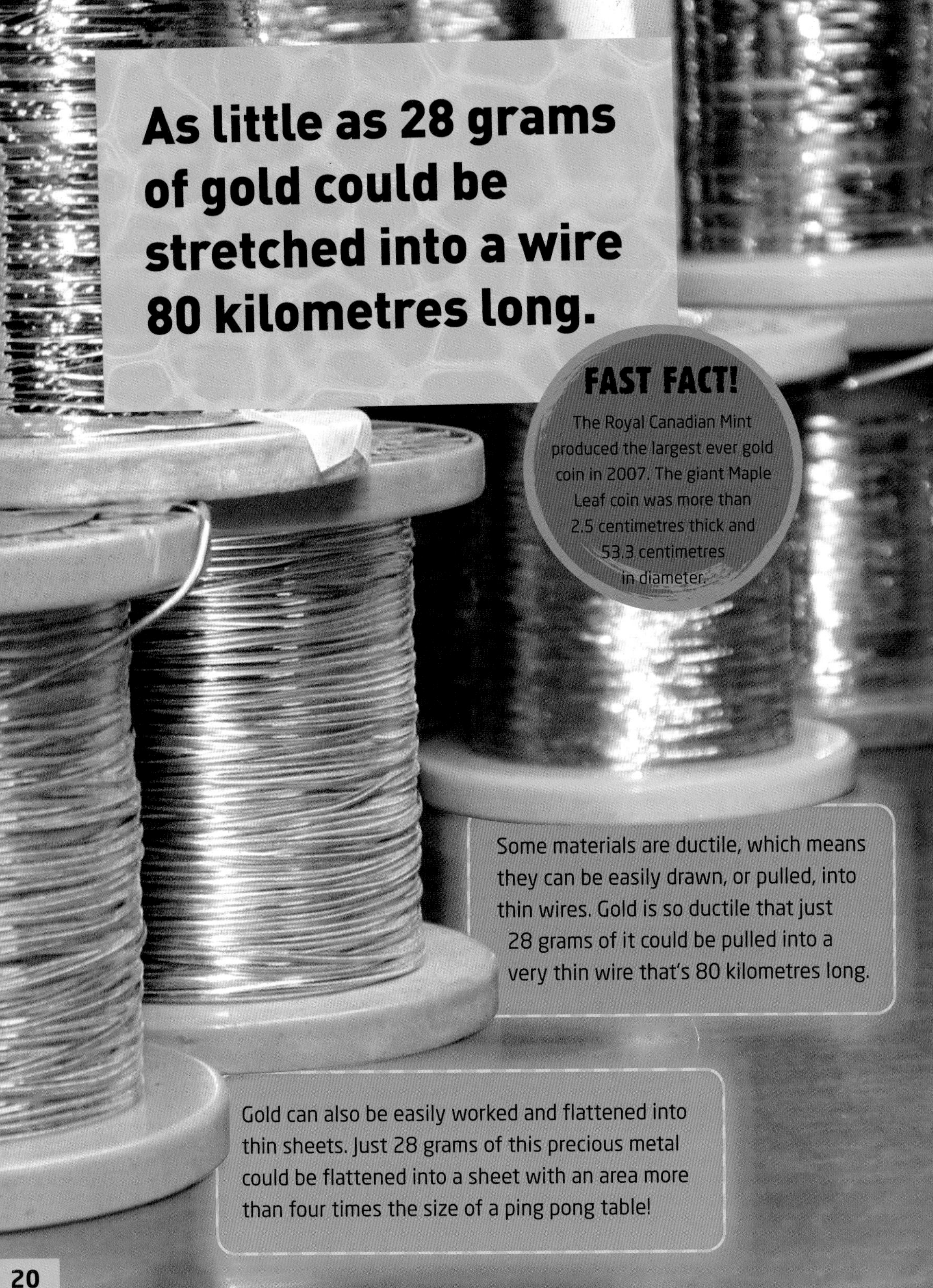

As little as 28 grams of gold could be stretched into a wire 80 kilometres long.

FAST FACT!

The Royal Canadian Mint produced the largest ever gold coin in 2007. The giant Maple Leaf coin was more than 2.5 centimetres thick and 53.3 centimetres in diameter.

Some materials are ductile, which means they can be easily drawn, or pulled, into thin wires. Gold is so ductile that just 28 grams of it could be pulled into a very thin wire that's 80 kilometres long.

Gold can also be easily worked and flattened into thin sheets. Just 28 grams of this precious metal could be flattened into a sheet with an area more than four times the size of a ping pong table!

Blame It on the Boogie, a hit song for The Jackson 5 featuring Michael Jackson, was written by a different Michael Jackson.

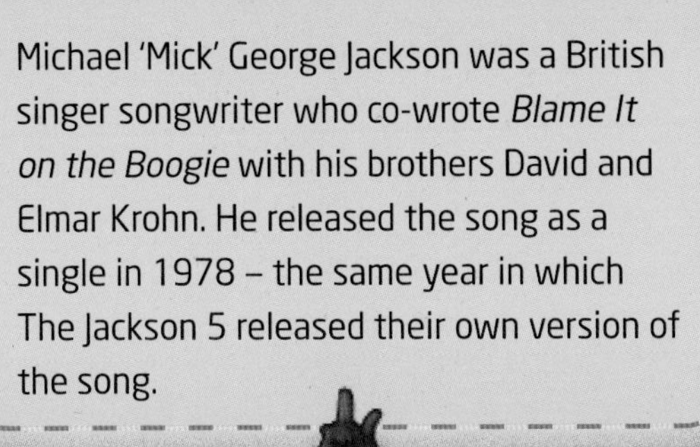

Michael 'Mick' George Jackson was a British singer songwriter who co-wrote *Blame It on the Boogie* with his brothers David and Elmar Krohn. He released the song as a single in 1978 – the same year in which The Jackson 5 released their own version of the song.

FAST FACT!

Mick Jackson was originally hoping to sell the song to Stevie Wonder.

Diplomats' shoes were bugged by spies in the 1960s.

In the 1960s, the United States and its allies were locked in secret spying battles with the Soviet Union and its supporters. The Czech secret service was on the side of the Soviets. Sometimes they would secretly intercept shoes ordered by American diplomats working in Czechoslovakia, fit a small bug inside the heel and deliver the shoes. The bugs would relay conversations to Czech spies nearby, using special listening equipment.

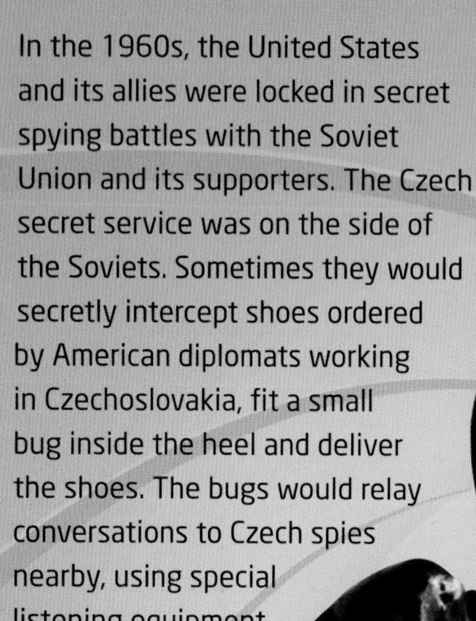

FAST FACT!

During the 1960s and 1970s, bugs were hidden in trees, in electrical sockets and behind mirrors. One radio transmitter was shaped like dog poo!

The biggest known win in an adult football game was 149–0.

The game was played in the Madagascan League between Stade Olympique l'Emyrne, known as SOE, and newly-crowned league champions AS Adema. SOE were upset at a refereeing decision in a previous match against AS Adema, and as a protest, started scoring own goals.

FAST FACT!

The biggest win in an international football game was Australia's 2001 win against American Samoa. The score was 31-0.

In football, if your team lets in a goal, you get the ball back to restart play with a kick-off. AS Adema's players never got a kick as their opponents kept scoring – 149 own goals in the 90-minute match. After the game, SOE's coach was suspended for three years.

More than 10 billion Android apps have been downloaded.

FAST FACT!

Google has named different versions of the Android operating system after cakes and desserts, including Cupcake, Ice Cream Sandwich and Gingerbread.

Android is an operating system – a set of programs that control how a digital device such as a personal computer or mobile phone works.

Android was first released in 2008. It became popular because you could download small computer programs called apps (short for applications) to perform dozens of different tasks, from getting a weather forecast to playing games or music. Many of the apps available are free, and by 2011 more than 10 billion had been downloaded.

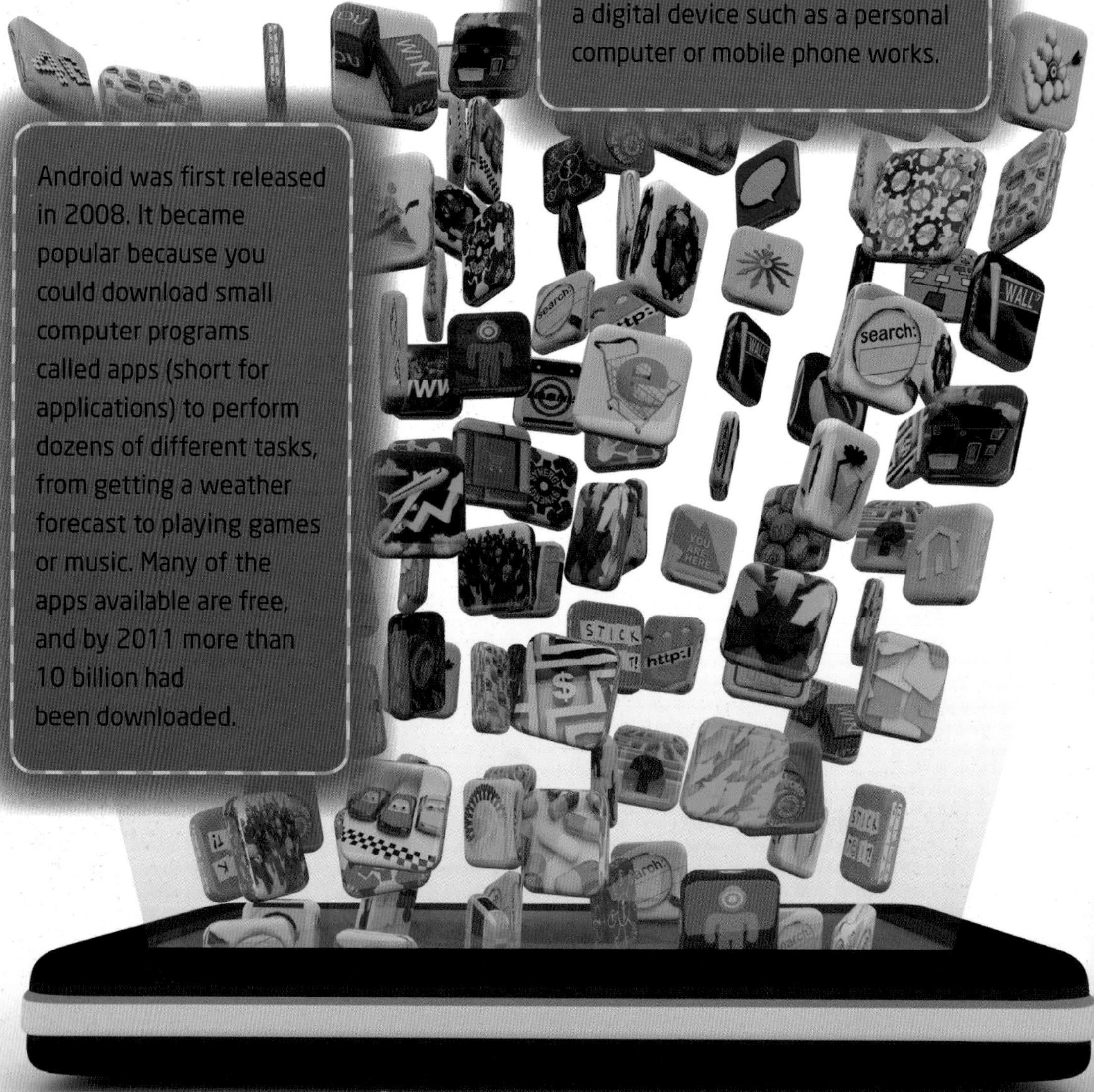

Before he became US president, Andrew Jackson shot and killed a man in a duel.

FAST FACT!

Danish astronomer Tycho Brahe lost part of his nose in a sword duel. He is said to have worn a false nose made of silver, gold and wax for much of his life.

In 1806, a lawyer called Charles Dickinson took part in a duel with Andrew Jackson (who became the seventh president of the United States in 1828). The pair had quarrelled in Tennessee, but as that state had outlawed duelling, they crossed the state line to fight in Kentucky.

JACKSON

Jackson's single shot struck Dickinson in the chest and killed him. Dickinson's shot hit Jackson in the chest as well, but he survived. The bullet lodged close to his heart and remained inside his body for the rest of his life.

Heavyweight boxing champ George Foreman has five sons, all called George.

FAST FACT!

George Foreman won his first 40 professional fights before losing to Muhammad Ali in Kinshasa, Zaire.

American George Foreman is a boxing legend. He won an Olympic gold medal as a heavyweight as far back as 1968, and five years later knocked out Joe Frazier to become heavyweight champion of the world. In 1994, at the age of 45, he became the oldest heavyweight champion again when he defeated Michael Moorer. As well as naming his five sons George, Foreman also named one of his daughters Georgetta!

Every three seconds a ladies' handbag is sold on eBay.

eBay began life as a simple auction website created by Pierre Omidyar back in 1995. The first item sold on eBay was Omidyar's old laser pen, which went for about £10 despite being broken.

FAST FACT!

EBay is used to buy and sell all sorts of things. Some weird items listed in the past include a lunch with business magnate Warren Buffet, a jet plane and puppies!

eBay is now ENORMOUS. In 2011, £4100-worth of goods were sold on the US version of eBay every second. Globally, a handbag is sold on eBay every 3 seconds, a laptop computer every 2 minutes and a mobile phone every 21 seconds.

Mercury is the closest planet to the Sun, yet temperatures can drop to as low as -173°C.

Mercury is the smallest planet in the Solar System – at 5300 kilometres in diameter. Its orbit takes it as close as 46.5 million kilometres from the Sun. If you could stand on Mercury's surface the Sun would look two-and-a-half times bigger in the sky than it does on Earth. When the Sun sets on Mercury, the temperature plummets because it lacks any atmosphere to trap heat.

FAST FACT!

Mercury's gravity is much lower than Earth's. If you weighed 45 kilograms on Earth, then you would weigh about 17 kilograms on Mercury.

The first microchip in 1971 held 2300 transistors. A recent chip holds 2600 million!

FAST FACT!

American Robert Noyce co-founded the companies Fairchild Semiconductor and Intel. He helped invent the microchip, gaining the nickname 'Mayor of Silicon Valley'!

Transistors are a crucial component used in computers and other electronic devices. In 1971, engineers managed to shrink transistors onto a single wafer of silicon to produce the first microprocessor – a device that can act as the central processing unit (CPU) of a computer.

Transistor shrinking has continued at a rapid rate, creating much faster and more powerful chips and personal computers as a result.

The first ever aircraft flight covered a distance of less than half the length of some modern passenger planes.

FAST FACT!

The entire Wright Flyer aircraft weighed just 274 kilograms. Its engine generated just 12 horsepower – less than a sixth of a family car's engine today.

In 1903, at Kill Devil Hills in North Carolina, USA, Orville Wright made the first successful aircraft flight, with his brother Wilbur watching from the ground. The 12-second flight saw the Wright Flyer travel just 36.5 metres – a third of the length of a football pitch and less than half the length of a Boeing 747-8I.

The world's biggest beaver dam is 850 metres long and can be viewed from space by satellites.

FAST FACT!

Beaver teeth grow continuously to counter their constant chomping on wood.

Built by generations of beavers, the world's largest beaver dam was found in 2007 using satellite images taken from space. The dam, which is in an isolated part of Wood Buffalo National Park in Northern Alberta, Canada, may have taken 40 years to construct to its current size. It is longer than eight football pitches and twice as long as the Hoover Dam.

A 13-year-old boy wrote the first commercial website about football.

FAST FACT!

Maddie Bradshaw from Texas, USA, invented decorated bottle top magnets. She sold them through her company, M3 Girl Designs, and became a millionaire by the age of 13.

English schoolboy Tom Hadfield first used the Internet back in 1994, long before there were many sites on the World Wide Web. He realized that lots of people all over the world wanted to know the results of major football games, so he created the Soccernet website the following year.

In 1999, when Tom was only 17, Soccernet was sold to ESPN for a cool £26.5 million. Not too bad for a teen, eh?

Sliced bread was once banned in the United States.

On 18 January 1943, the head of the American War Foods Administration banned pre-sliced bread. The Second World War was raging and it was thought that banning sliced bread would save paper as thick sheets of it were used to hold all the slices of a cut loaf together. The ban was far from popular and didn't last long. Less than two months later it was lifted!

FAST FACT!

In 2011, 50 chefs in Mexico created one of the world's biggest sandwiches – a ham and cheese monster measuring more than 52.7 metres in length.

The largest meteorite ever found weighed 54,431 kilograms.

Meteorites are fragments of rock from outer space, which survive travelling through Earth's atmosphere and reach our planet's surface. Most are pretty small, but the specimen found in 1920 at Hoba West in the African country of Namibia was a whopper. Scientists believe it fell more than 80,000 years ago.

FAST FACT!

Many scientists believe that more than a dozen meteorites found in Antarctica originally came from Mars.

Meteorites fall every year on Earth, and in 2009, German teenager Gerrit Blank was hit on the hand by a small meteorite while walking home. He survived to tell the tale.

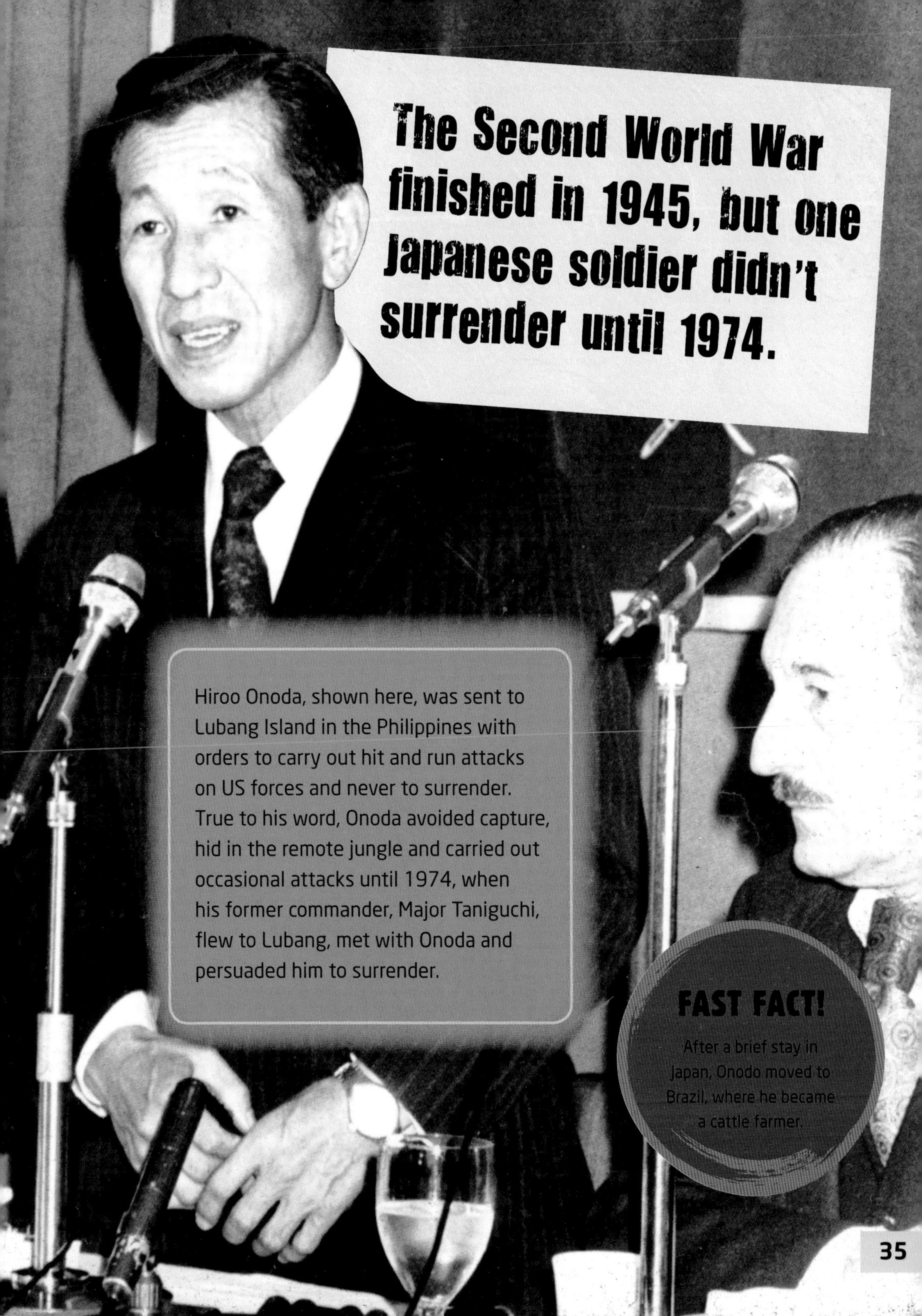

The Second World War finished in 1945, but one Japanese soldier didn't surrender until 1974.

Hiroo Onoda, shown here, was sent to Lubang Island in the Philippines with orders to carry out hit and run attacks on US forces and never to surrender. True to his word, Onoda avoided capture, hid in the remote jungle and carried out occasional attacks until 1974, when his former commander, Major Taniguchi, flew to Lubang, met with Onoda and persuaded him to surrender.

FAST FACT!

After a brief stay in Japan, Onodo moved to Brazil, where he became a cattle farmer.

The blue whale's heart is as big as a small car.

Blue whales are huge! The biggest can grow to more than 30 metres in length and weigh over 181,437 kilograms. Their hearts are the size of a Volkswagen Beetle car, and can weigh up to 590 kilograms. The heart pumps blood through the arteries, some of which are more than 20 centimetres wide. Want one more blue whale wonder fact? Its heartbeat can be heard up to 3.2 kilometres away.

FAST FACT!

A blue whale's heart beats only five or six times a minute, but it pumps more than 9 tonnes of blood through the whale's body.

Ice speedway riders race on motorbikes without brakes, and with tyres covered in spikes.

FAST FACT!

There are usually 180 to 200 spikes on the rear wheel of an ice speedway motorbike.

Ice Speedway is an exciting form of motorcycle racing around a short oval track covered in ice, usually less than 457 metres in length.

The bike tyres are covered in sharp steel spikes, each up to 3.2 centimetres long. These spikes grip the ice and propel the bike forwards. Riders reach top speeds of 130 to 145 kph on the straight sections, then angle and slide their bikes around the slippery bends. Awesome!

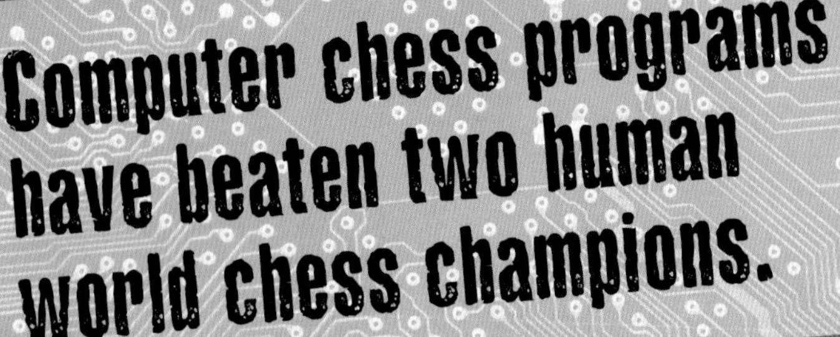

Computer chess programs have beaten two human world chess champions.

In 2006, Vladimir Kramnik was the undisputed chess champion of the world. He took on the Deep Fritz chess computer program and lost. The first world champion to lose to a computer was Garry Kasparov in 1997. He lost to IBM's Deep Blue computer. Deep Blue could check out 200 million chess positions per second.

FAST FACT!

Invented in 1770, the Turk – a machine that played chess – caused a sensation, but it turned out that a human was hidden inside.

Astronauts grow taller in space.

FAST FACT!

Astronauts' footprints will stay on the surface of the Moon for millions of years because there is no wind to blow them away.

An astronaut's body goes through many stresses and strains in space, especially when staying on a space station for months at a time. Gravity in space is far less than it is on Earth, which means that the forces pressing down on the spine are greatly reduced, allowing the vertebrae in your spine to spread apart a little.

Space station astronauts can grow as much as 5 centimetres taller, but after some time back on Earth they go back to their usual height.

Futility, a story about a giant ship called *Titan* which sinks in the Atlantic after striking an iceberg, was published 14 years before the real-life sinking of the *Titanic*.

FAST FACT!

When the *Titanic* sank, 1517 of the 2300 people believed to be on board died. That is almost two-thirds of the crew and passengers!

American author Morgan Robertson published his story *Futility* in 1898 and it has many spooky coincidences with the real *Titanic* disaster of 1912. Just like the *Titanic*, *Titan* was the biggest ship of its age and sank in the month of April. Both ships were powered by three propellers, had two masts and could carry a maximum of 3000 passengers. The *Titan* struck an iceberg at around midnight, while the *Titanic* struck an iceberg at 20 minutes to midnight.

U2 singer Bono spent £1000 to fly his favourite hat to him in time to go on stage.

Bono was on the way to a special charity concert in Modena, Italy, hosted by opera singer Luciano Pavarotti in 2003 when he realized he didn't have his favourite hat, a trilby, with him. The singer paid for a taxi to drive the hat to London's Gatwick Airport and then paid for a first-class seat on a flight from Gatwick to Bologna in Italy. Finally, he had to spend about £134 for a taxi to drive the hat from Bologna to Modena.

FAST FACT!

Another valuable hat is the one worn in the film *Indiana Jones and the Kingdom of the Crystal Skull*, which sold at a charity auction for £13,000.

The entire country of Monaco is about the same size as London's Hyde Park.

The principality of Monaco is surrounded by France and the Mediterranean Sea. It is only 347.4 metres wide in places and has a total area of 1.96 square kilometres. Hyde Park in London is only a little bit smaller than that at 1.42 square kilometres.

FAST FACT!

It takes less than an hour for an average person to walk across the entire country of Monaco.

The first successful expedition through the Grand Canyon was led by a one-armed war veteran.

Major John Wesley Powell was an avid explorer before taking part in the American Civil War where he lost most of his right arm at the Battle of Shiloh (1862).

Seven years later, Powell led a small party on an expedition. They travelled for more than 1600 kilometres down the Green and Colorado rivers to explore the enormous and, at the time, largely unexplored Grand Canyon.

FAST FACT!

It wasn't until Powell's second expedition in 1871 that the Grand Canyon was mapped.

Goodnight Moon author Margaret Wise Brown left her fortune to a nine-year-old neighbour.

US author Margaret Wise Brown wrote her first children's book, *When the Wind Blew*, in 1937. She wrote many children's bestsellers, such as *Goodnight Moon* and *The Runaway Bunny*, before dying at the age of 42. She left behind over 70 unpublished stories. In her will, she asked for the royalties from all her books, which over the years would total several million pounds, to go to Albert Clarke, the nine-year-old son of her neighbour in Maine, USA.

FAST FACT!

Goodnight Moon was one of former president George W. Bush's favourite childhood stories.

A shipwrecked man survived alone on a raft at sea for an incredible 133 days.

FAST FACT!

Alexander Selkirk, a sailor, was marooned on an uninhabited island in the Pacific Ocean in 1704. He had to wait for four years before being rescued.

Poon Lim was a Chinese steward onboard the *Ben Lomond*, a merchant (non-military) ship during the Second World War, when a submarine torpedo sank the vessel. Poon spent a staggering four months on a small wooden life raft floating in the Atlantic Ocean.

Poon Lim survived by catching the occasional fish, and by using the canvas covering of his lifejacket to harvest rainwater. He was finally rescued by Brazilian fishermen.

The ashes of the creator of *Star Trek* have flown into space twice.

Gene Roddenberry created the first *Star Trek* television series. When he died in 1991, his body was cremated, and some of his ashes were flown into space and back to Earth onboard a 1992 Space Shuttle mission. Five years later, a Celestis rocket was launched, carrying his ashes back into space again.

FAST FACT!

The original *Star Trek* series ran for three seasons, and was extended into several other shows such as *Star Trek: Voyager* and *Deep Space Nine*.

A mysterious explosion in 1908 flattened more than 80 million trees.

FAST FACT!

Some possible explanations for the explosion include a comet, a natural H-bomb, a black hole and antimatter getting into Earth's atmosphere.

The explosion occurred in Tunguska, a heavily forested part of Siberia, Russia. An area of about 2150 square kilometres was devastated, and shock waves travelled right around the Earth. To this day, scientists are not completely sure what caused the gigantic explosion.

Art students in London made a sculpture of King Kong entirely out of popcorn.

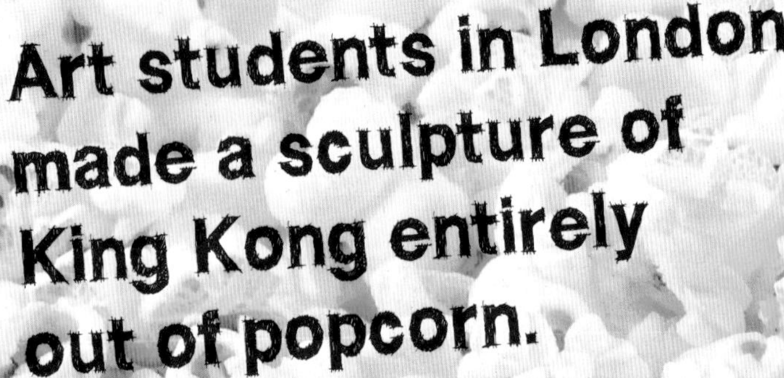

In 2003, students at the Camberwell College of Arts in London constructed a giant sculpture of the famous movie monster.

It took 630 hours to build the beast out of popcorn to celebrate the 70th anniversary of the first *King Kong* film. The finished sculpture stood 3.9 metres high and weighed more than 771 kilograms – the weight of four real gorillas.

FAST FACT!

Currently, the largest ever popcorn sculpture is a 5-layer cake that stood just under 6.4 metres tall and weighed 5300 kilograms!

One Australian coin became more valuable melted down for its silver than for the coin's face value.

FAST FACT!

The most expensive coin is the 'Flowing Hair dollar', which sold in 2005 for £5.06 million. It was minted, or made, in 1794 and 1795 as the first US dollar coin.

In 1966, a new Australian 50-cent piece was minted. The first coins were made of 80 per cent silver and 20 per cent copper, and were so large that three coins contained 28 grams of silver.

As the price of silver soared in the world markets, the amount of silver in the coin was worth as much as four times the face value of the coin. They were withdrawn as currency soon afterwards!

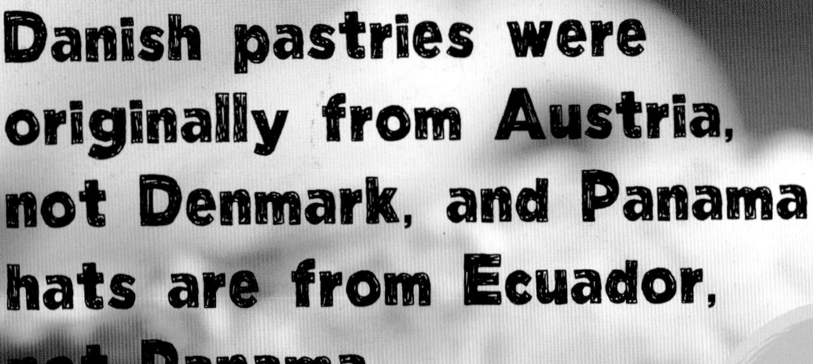

Danish pastries were originally from Austria, not Denmark, and Panama hats are from Ecuador, not Panama.

FAST FACT!

One of the first historical figures to wear a panama hat was French emperor and military leader Napoleon Bonaparte!

It's funny how some things get their names. The sweet pastries we call Danish were first baked in the Austrian city of Vienna. In the mid-19th century, Austrian bakers working in Denmark first introduced the pastry, where it was developed further and became known as a Danish.

The Panama hat is made from the woven leaves of the toquilla straw plant. These plants and hats actually come from Ecuador, but became known as Panama hats because many Americans, including President Theodore Roosevelt, bought the hats in Panama.

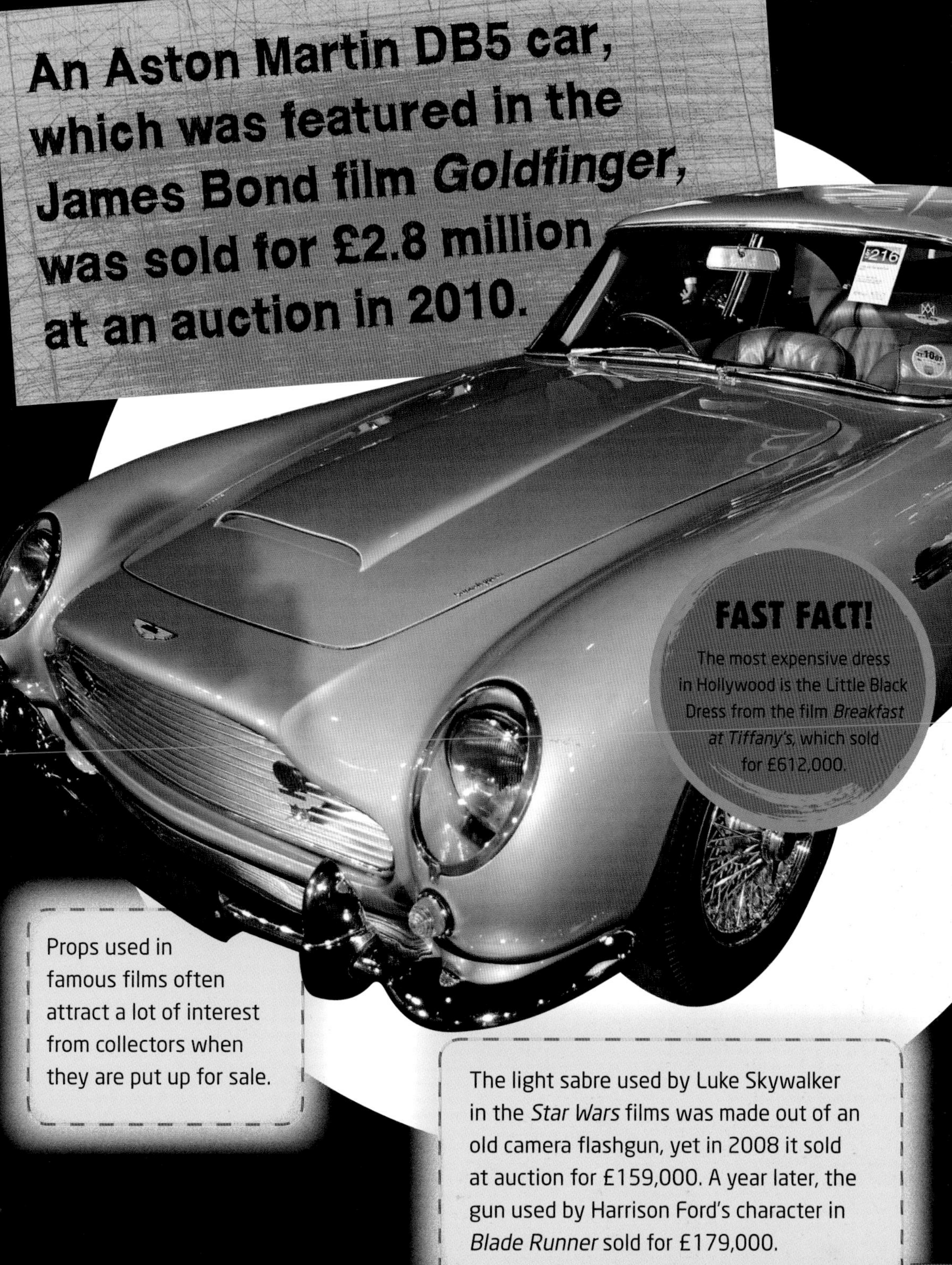

An Aston Martin DB5 car, which was featured in the James Bond film *Goldfinger*, was sold for £2.8 million at an auction in 2010.

FAST FACT!

The most expensive dress in Hollywood is the Little Black Dress from the film *Breakfast at Tiffany's*, which sold for £612,000.

Props used in famous films often attract a lot of interest from collectors when they are put up for sale.

The light sabre used by Luke Skywalker in the *Star Wars* films was made out of an old camera flashgun, yet in 2008 it sold at auction for £159,000. A year later, the gun used by Harrison Ford's character in *Blade Runner* sold for £179,000.

A man survived a jet airliner flight across the Atlantic Ocean stowed away in the wheel housing of the plane.

In 1969, 17-year-old Armando Socarras Ramirez sought to escape from Cuba by stowing away inside the wheel housing of a DC-8 jet airliner bound for Spain.

FAST FACT!

Ramirez stuffed his ears with cotton wool to muffle the engine noise and wore shoes with rubber soles to help him climb up inside the wheel housing.

Ramirez endured icy cold temperatures of -40°C and he struggled to get enough oxygen due to the thin air, but he survived the journey and the touchdown at an airport in Madrid, Spain.

At just one drip per second, a tap can leak 11,356 litres per year.

FAST FACT!

Water costs money to use – so if your tap is leaking, your money is literally going down the drain!

If you care about not wasting water, get your parents to fix any dripping taps in your house as the water they waste builds up quickly. Lots of water is wasted at home due to leaking hose connections too, but these drips are dwarfed by leaks in city water supply pipes.

According to *The New York Times*, the New York City water supply system loses 99 million litres per year due to leaks.

An Alaska moose's antlers weigh more than a typical seven-year-old boy.

Alaska, or giant, moose live in Alaska, USA, and parts of northern Canada. They are the largest of all moose, standing over 2 metres tall from hoof to shoulder, and reaching 2.7 metres in length.

FAST FACT!

Alaska moose have tough tongues. They have been known to use them to lick salt off the roads in icy weather.

A male moose's antlers can span more than 1.8 metres and weigh over 27 kilograms. They are shed at the end of each year, and a new pair grows the following year.

Glaciers hold around 70 per cent of all the fresh water on Earth.

FAST FACT!

According to the National Snow and Ice Data Center, in Washington State, USA, melting glaciers provide a staggering 2130 litres of water.

Glaciers are giant bodies of ice that cover almost ten per cent of the world's land. They are packed full of fresh water and are mostly found in the polar regions. Glaciers are also found in the high mountain ranges of many continent, from the Alps in Europe to the Rocky Mountains in the United States. According to the British Geological Society, if all the glacier ice melted, the world's seas would rise significantly.

Forces generated by a Formula One car would allow it to drive on a ceiling.

A Formula One (F1) car is one of the most advanced racing vehicles in the world. Its body generates a lot of downforce – a force which helps push the car's tyres onto the track to improve grip.

FAST FACT!

A Formula One car's engine and brakes are so powerful that the vehicle can go from zero to 160 kilometres per hour and back in just 5.5 seconds.

At speeds of above 193 kilometres per hour, an F1 car generates more force than its own weight, which means that in theory, it could drive upside down without falling to the ground.

A South American bird barks instead of sings.

The Jocotoco Antpitta bird was discovered in 1997, in a remote part of the Andes mountain range of South America. Discovered by scientist Robert Ridgely, it is one of the largest new birds to be discovered in the past 50 years. It is about 20 to 23 centimetres in length, with long legs for hopping around the rainforest floor.

The Jocotoco Antpitta bird's call is deeper than most other birds, and sounds more like a small dog's bark than birdsong.

FAST FACT!

A Jocotoco Antpitta eats worms, ants and other insects. Its bark is worse than it's bite; they are actually shy birds.

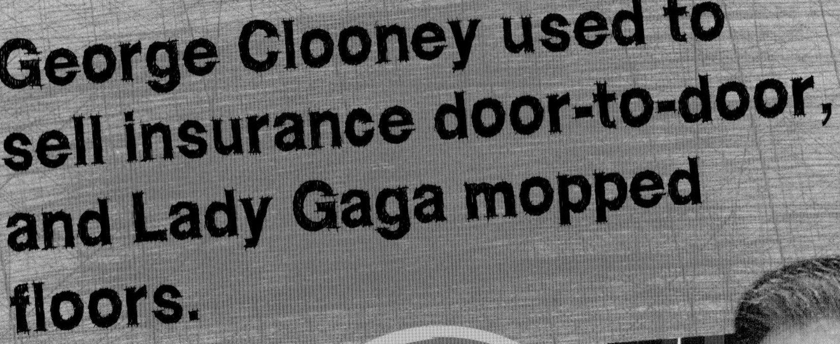

George Clooney used to sell insurance door-to-door, and Lady Gaga mopped floors.

FAST FACT!

One of Brad Pitt's first ever jobs was wearing a large chicken suit and dancing around to attract potential customers into a chicken restaurant in Los Angeles, USA.

Before becoming a pop music sensation, Lady Gaga (then known as Stephani Germanotta), worked as a waitress, serving customers and mopping floors at a Greek restaurant in New York City, USA.

Clooney tried out for professional baseball with the Cincinnati Reds, but when that didn't work out, he worked selling men's suits, insurance and as a tobacco harvester before getting his big break in the TV series, *ER*.

A million American one-dollar bills weigh over 900 kilograms.

The US dollar bill is 15.5 cm long, 6.6 cm wide and is 0.01 cm thick. Over 40 per cent of all bills printed in the US are one dollar bills.

Each bill weighs just over 8.5 g, so a million of them stacked together would weigh around 925 kg and make a pile 103 m high. As $100 bills are the same thickness and weight as single dollar bills, a million dollars in $100s would weigh about 9.25 kg.

FAST FACT!

The heaviest coin was produced by Canada. It consists of 99.99% gold, is 50 centimetres wide and weighs a total of 99 kilograms.

Among the crazy weapons of World War II was a gun that could fire around corners and, planned but not used, bats fitted with bombs.

The *Krummlauf*, or 'curved barrel' in English, was a bent barrel fitted to a German Sturmgewehr 44 assault rifle so soldiers could fire around corners in close combat.

The American forces, in contrast, tested out but didn't deploy, the idea of dropping thousands of Mexican free-tailed bats fitted with firebombs into Japanese towns, many of which were largely constructed of wooden buildings.

FAST FACT!

Other animals that were used during wartime include dolphins, rats, cats and dogs.

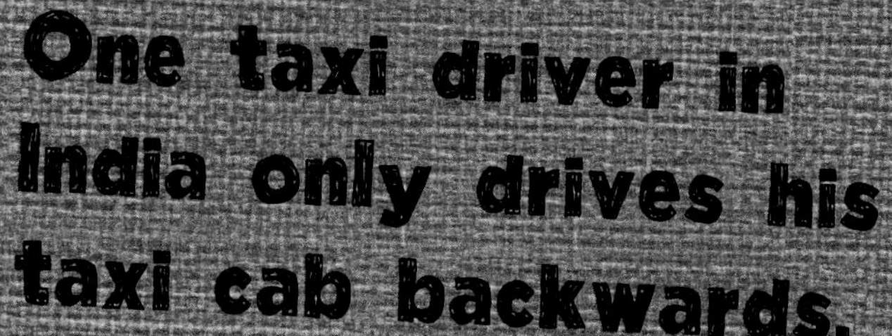

One taxi driver in India only drives his taxi cab backwards.

FAST FACT!

in 1907, New York businessman Harry N. Allen was the first to paint his taxis yellow as this colour made the vehicles more visible.

Harpeet Devi drove his taxi cab in Punjab, India, in a regular way until his car gearbox got stuck and would only work in reverse. While saving up to have the gearbox fixed, Devi drove the cab backwards. He got to like it so much that he actually had his car converted to drive backwards, with four reverse gears and a special siren to warn other motorists!

If Earth's history were shrunk into 24 hours then humans first appeared less than two minutes before the end of the last hour.

FAST FACT!

One of the oldest pieces of art we know of is the Venus of Hohle Fels, found in Germany. Carved from a mammoth tusk, the figure is believed to be up to 40,000 years old.

Earth was formed approximately 4.54 billion years ago, but homo sapiens - human beings as we know them - were pretty late arrivals. Scientists estimate that humans started developing 150,000 to 200,000 years ago. So if Earth's history started at 0:00 and ran for 24 hours, then humans arrived later than 11:58 p.m - two minutes to midnight.

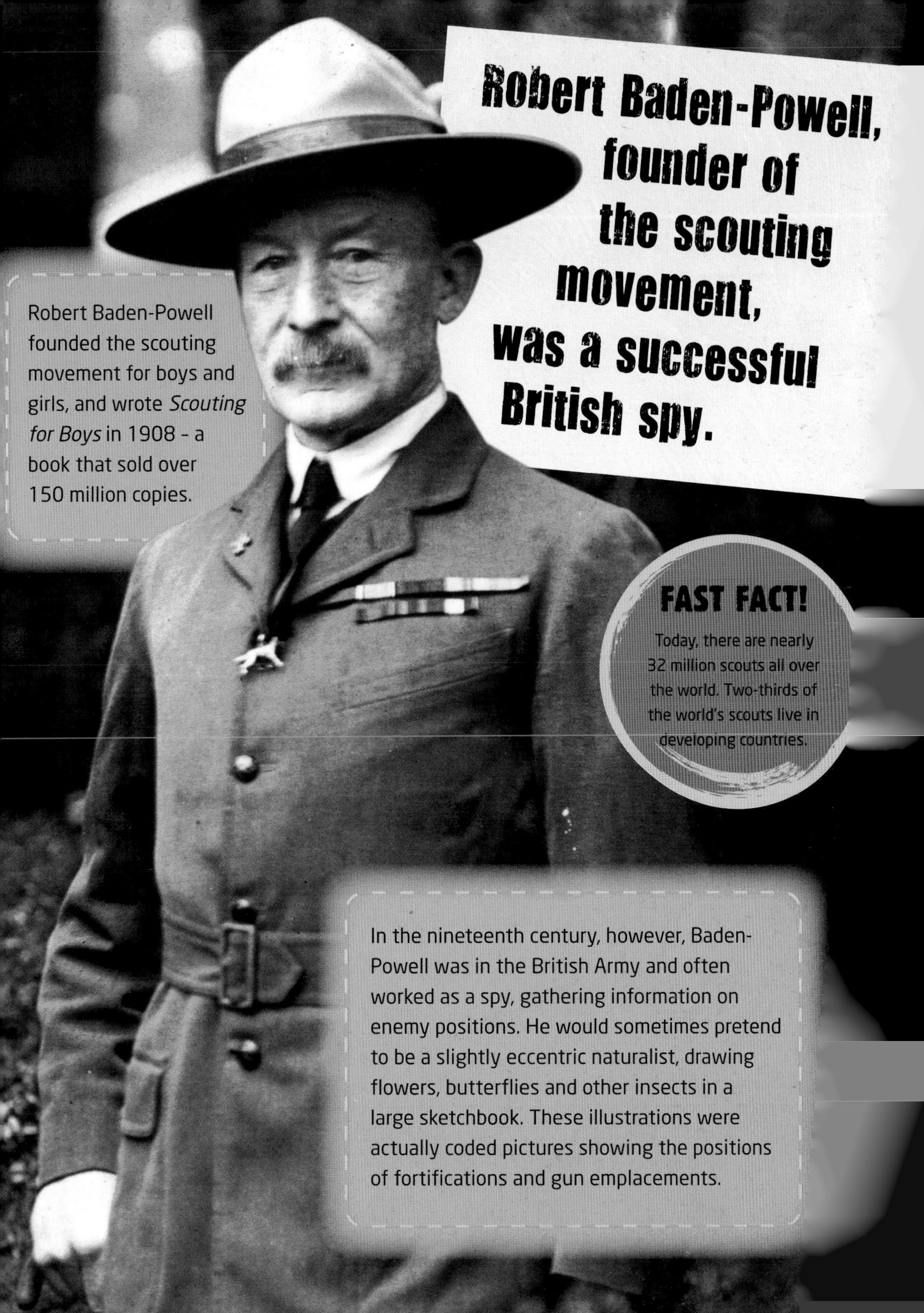

Robert Baden-Powell, founder of the scouting movement, was a successful British spy.

Robert Baden-Powell founded the scouting movement for boys and girls, and wrote *Scouting for Boys* in 1908 – a book that sold over 150 million copies.

FAST FACT!

Today, there are nearly 32 million scouts all over the world. Two-thirds of the world's scouts live in developing countries.

In the nineteenth century, however, Baden-Powell was in the British Army and often worked as a spy, gathering information on enemy positions. He would sometimes pretend to be a slightly eccentric naturalist, drawing flowers, butterflies and other insects in a large sketchbook. These illustrations were actually coded pictures showing the positions of fortifications and gun emplacements.

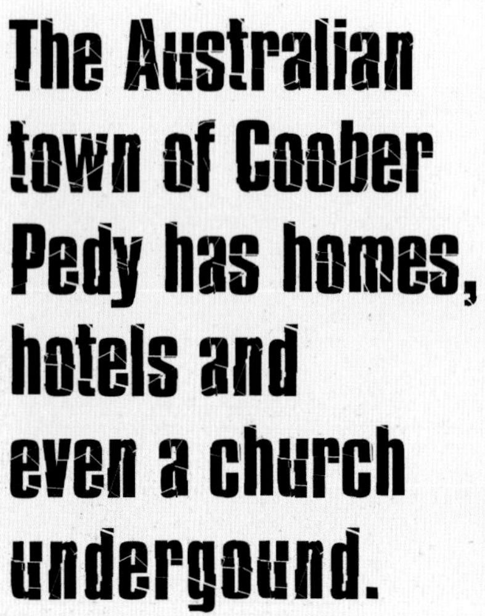

The Australian town of Coober Pedy has homes, hotels and even a church undergound.

Coober Pedy is a small Australian mining town famous for producing most of the world's opal gemstones. About half of its 3000 residents live underground in homes burrowed out of the rock, as life beneath the surface is cooler than the desert heat above. There is also an underground church – St Peter and Paul's Catholic Church – and even an underground campsite where visitors can pitch their tents.

FAST FACT!

Coober Pedy's golf course is made up of sand, not grass.

Batman's car in the original TV series was made from a concept car that was bought for only one dollar (66 pence).

FAST FACT!

The producers of the show had seat belts installed into the Batmobile to address complaints from the American National Safety Council.

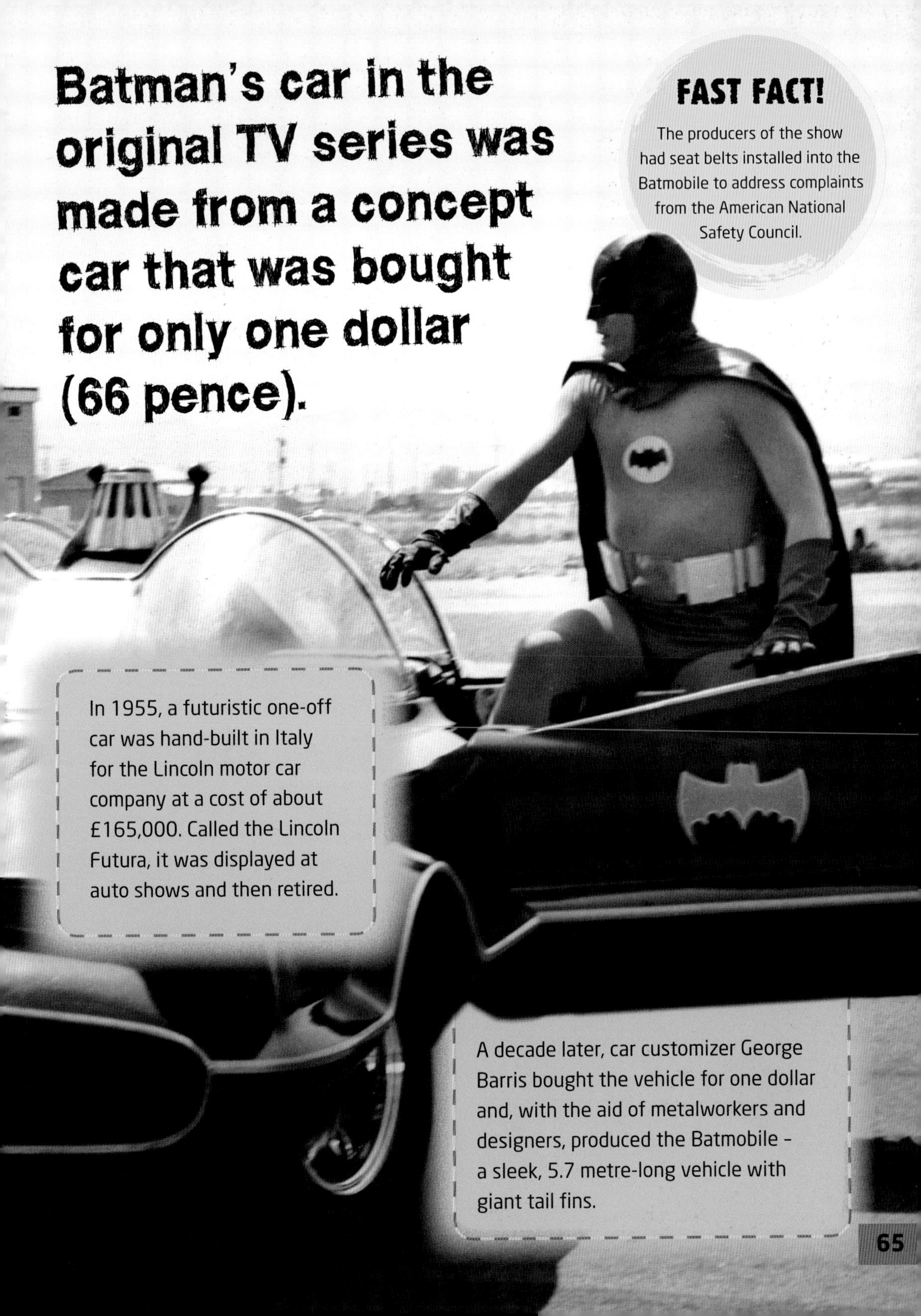

In 1955, a futuristic one-off car was hand-built in Italy for the Lincoln motor car company at a cost of about £165,000. Called the Lincoln Futura, it was displayed at auto shows and then retired.

A decade later, car customizer George Barris bought the vehicle for one dollar and, with the aid of metalworkers and designers, produced the Batmobile – a sleek, 5.7 metre-long vehicle with giant tail fins.

Taisto Miettinen was World Wife-Carrying Champion in 2009, 2010 and 2011.

The World Wife-Carrying Championships began in the small town of Sonkajärvi in Finland in the mid-1990s. The competition involves racing around a course, often including obstacles such as water jumps, with men carrying their wives or partners over their shoulders.

Taisto Miettinen is a Finnish lawyer who has become three-times world champion. The 2011 event was watched by a crowd of over 6000 spectators and featured 43 racers from 10 different countries.

FAST FACT!

The Wife-Carrying world record is 55.5 seconds, set by an Estonian couple in 2001.

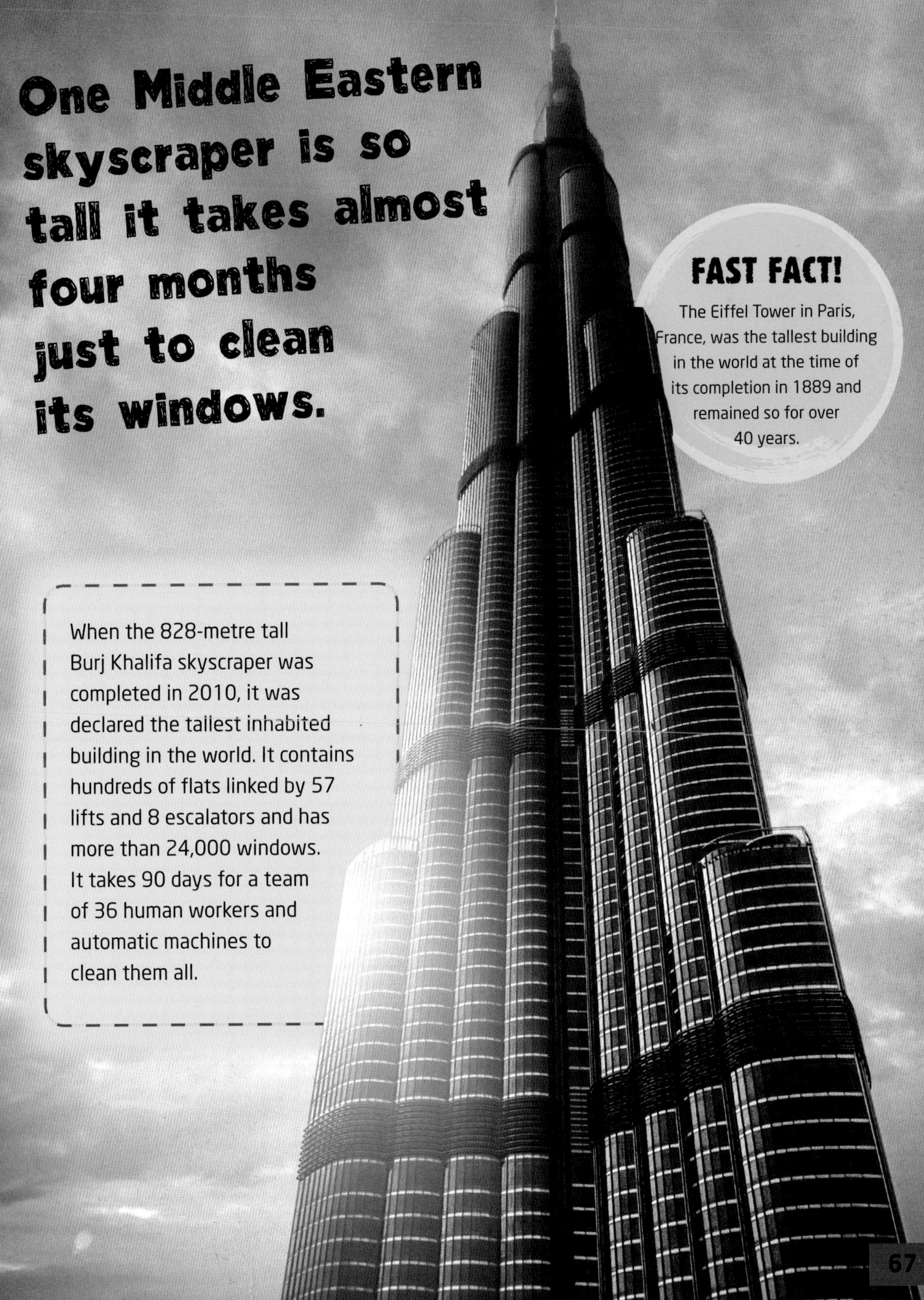

One Middle Eastern skyscraper is so tall it takes almost four months just to clean its windows.

FAST FACT!

The Eiffel Tower in Paris, France, was the tallest building in the world at the time of its completion in 1889 and remained so for over 40 years.

When the 828-metre tall Burj Khalifa skyscraper was completed in 2010, it was declared the tallest inhabited building in the world. It contains hundreds of flats linked by 57 lifts and 8 escalators and has more than 24,000 windows. It takes 90 days for a team of 36 human workers and automatic machines to clean them all.

The world's smallest production car, the Peel P50, weighed less than its driver.

Built between 1962 and 1965, the Peel P50 was tiny, measuring 1.4 metres long, 1 metre wide and 1.1 metre high. It weighed a mere 59.5 kg – less than most adult drivers – and was powered by a puny 49cc moped engine, giving the car a top speed of less than 64 kph. Parking, though, was easy. Drivers just got out of the car and pulled it into position by hand!

FAST FACT!

In 2010, a new replica of the Peel P50 was built. It was powered by a tiny electric motor which gave the vehicle a top speed of just 16 kph.

Homer, Marge, Lisa and Maggie are the real-life first names of *The Simpsons*' creator Matt Groening's father, mother and two sisters.

FAST FACT!

There have been more guest stars on *The Simpsons* than there are episodes. Maggie's first and only word was guest voiced by actress Elizabeth Taylor.

Matt Groening's funny cartoon family first appeared on television in 1987 as short excerpts in the *Tracy Ullman Show*. Two years later, it became a full-length show in its own right and proved an instant hit. Over 500 episodes have been made, winning 27 Emmy awards. It has now become the longest continually running sitcom on American TV.

It's free to post letters inside Andorra.

FAST FACT!
The most valuable stamp in the world is worth £1.4 million. It is a Swedish stamp called the Treskillin Yellow and was printed in 1855.

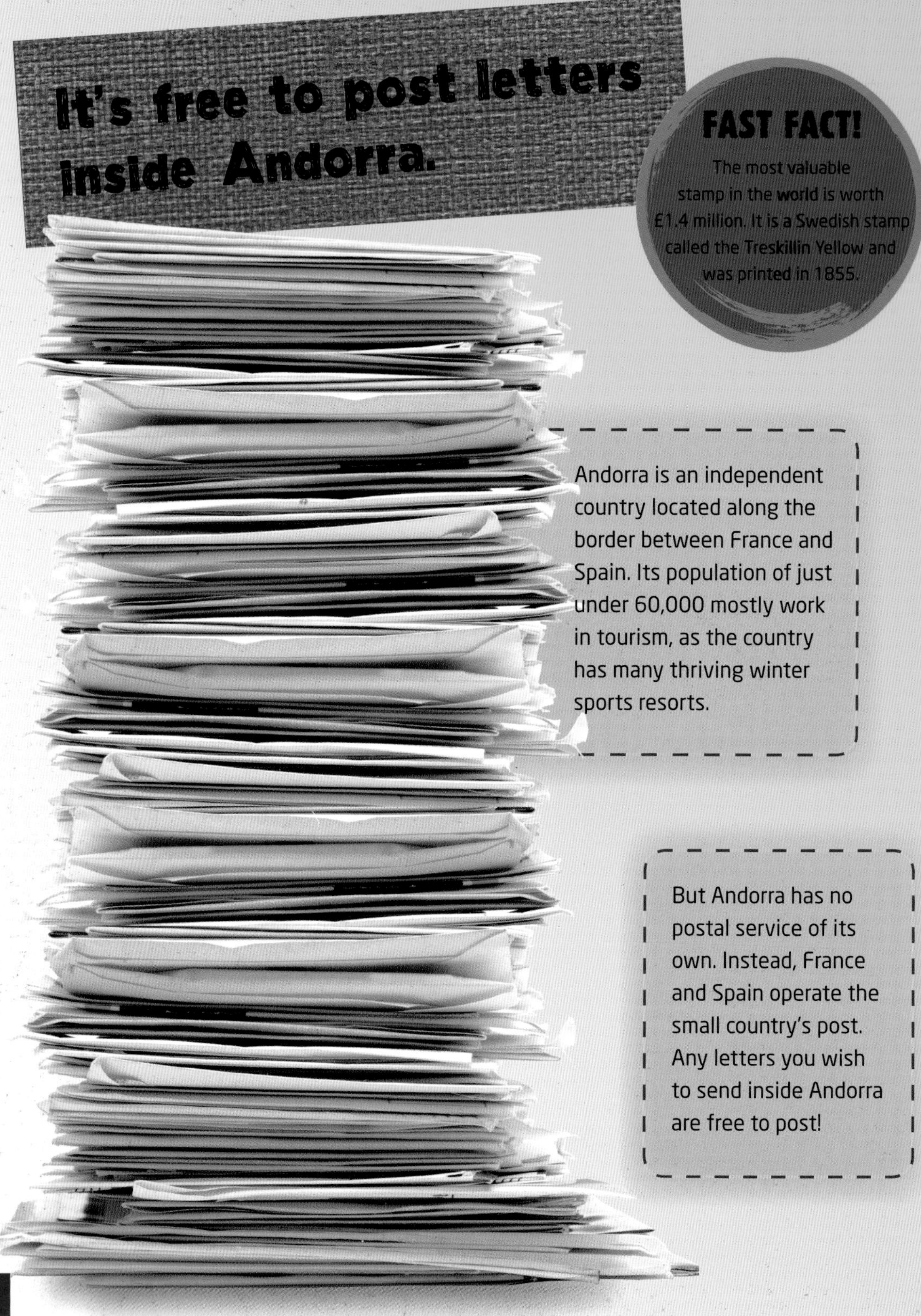

Andorra is an independent country located along the border between France and Spain. Its population of just under 60,000 mostly work in tourism, as the country has many thriving winter sports resorts.

But Andorra has no postal service of its own. Instead, France and Spain operate the small country's post. Any letters you wish to send inside Andorra are free to post!

Ancient Egyptian pharaoh Tutankhamen was buried with 32 pairs of sandals and 139 walking sticks.

When an expedition led by Howard Carter unearthed Tutankhamen's tomb in the 1920s, they got quite a surprise! Apart from the magnificent funeral coffin housing his body, Tutankhamen's tomb was packed with thousands of objects including ostrich feather fans, a bronze trumpet, a gold dagger, 30 jars of wine and six full-sized chariots.

FAST FACT!

Tutankhamen became pharaoh when he was only nine years old. A total of over 3000 treasures were placed in his tomb for his afterlife.

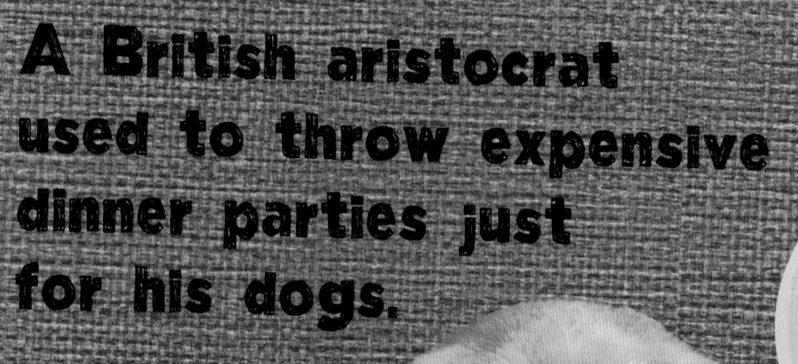

A British aristocrat used to throw expensive dinner parties just for his dogs.

FAST FACT!

Egerton died unmarried and without children, but was one of the richest men in the United Kingdom.

Francis Egerton was born in 1756 and became the 8th Earl of Bridgewater in 1823. He sat at the dinner table with his dogs as he preferred dogs to people. Each dog was dressed in fashionable clothes and was attended by its own human servant.

Egerton wore a pair of shoes only once, leaving them in rows so that he could tell how many days had passed.

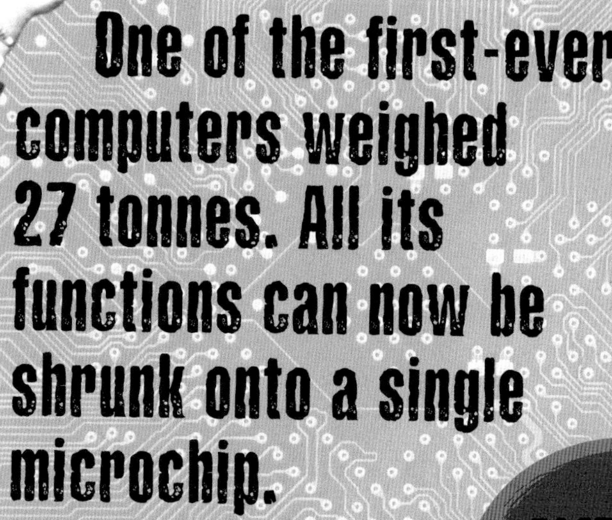

One of the first-ever computers weighed 27 tonnes. All its functions can now be shrunk onto a single microchip.

FAST FACT!

HP, Google, Microsoft and Apple are all very successful IT companies, but they were all started in people's garages.

The computer in question was the Electronic Numerical Integrator and Computer (or ENIAC, for short) completed in 1946 at the University of Pennsylvania's Moore School of Engineering. This beast of a machine consisted of banks of circuits and measured 24 metres long, 2.4 metres high and about 1 metre deep.

In 1996, computer scientists at the University of Pennsylvania built their own version of ENIAC on a silicon microchip the size of your fingernail.

US President William Taft was so tone deaf that he had to be nudged when the American national anthem was played so that he could stand up.

Taft, the 27th President of the United States from 1909 to 1915, holds a number of notable firsts. These include being the first President to own a car and the first person to be the head of two branches of the American government, when he became Chief Justice of the Supreme Court in 1921. He was also the last President to keep a cow (his was called Pauline) on the White House lawn.

FAST FACT!

President Taft was so large (he weighed over 136 kilograms) he needed a new, bigger bath after he got stuck in the first one.

An Olympic rower lost his gold medal in the lake on which he won the competition.

In 1956, Soviet Union rower Vyacheslav Ivanov won the single sculls race at the Melbourne Olympics in Australia. The 18-year old was delighted, then dismayed, as he accidentally dropped his gold medal into Lake Wendouree after the medal ceremony.

FAST FACT!

Ivanov was the first man to win the Olympic single sculls race three times in a row – 1956, 1960 and 1964.

The authorities took pity on Ivanov, and later presented him with a substitute gold medal.

In 2006, a man bought an original copy of the Declaration of Independence from an American charity shop for just £1.65.

FAST FACT!

The original Declaration is housed in a heavily-guarded, bullet-proof case. When the Archives are closed, the Declaration is moved to an underground vault.

Michael Sparks, a musical equipment technician, bought several items from a charity shop in Nashville, USA, – salt and pepper pots, a candleholder and what he thought was a modern reprint of the Declaration of Independence.

His 'reprint' turned out to be one of the 200 copies (of which only around 30 survive) of the official document printed in 1823. The following year, Sparks put it up for auction where it was sold for £316,850. Quite a profit!

Crickets hear through their knees.

Crickets are insects known for the chirping sound the males make by rubbing their wings together. There are over 900 different species of cricket. What is less well known is that crickets have a form of eardrum or, to give it its scientific term, tympanic membrane, located just below the middle joint of each front leg. These act as ears, allowing a cricket to hear other crickets.

FAST FACT!

Male crickets have a courting song to attract and impress nearby females.

American Ashrita Furman holds over 120 world records, including the longest distance travelled on a pogo stick.

FAST FACT!
Want more of Furman's feats? In 2007, he performed the most forward rolls in an hour (1330) and in 2010 he built the largest see-saw at over 24 metres long.

Ashrita Furman just cannot help himself. The health food shop manager from New York broke his first world record in 1979 and has broken 399 records since.

His achievements include creating the largest lollipop (2955 kilograms) in 2008 and, in 2011, eating the most mashed potatoes in a minute (677 grams).

In 2010, retail chain Walmart's income was greater than the entire economy of Norway.

FAST FACT!

If Walmart were a country it would be the 26th-largest economy in the world.

Walmart employs over 2 million people around the world. The company's income in 2010 was a whooping £278.38 billion. One measure of a country's economy is gross domestic product, or GDP for short.

The GDP is the value of all the goods and services produced in a country in a year. Norway's GDP for 2010 was estimated by the World Bank as £276.61 billion.

Lyndon B. Johnson, Sting, Stephen King, J.K. Rowling and Billy Crystal all worked as schoolteachers before they were famous.

Singer Sting used to teach at a convent school in Northumberland, while Stephen King wrote his famous novel, *Salem's Lot*, at night while working as a teacher at Hampden Academy in Maine, USA.

Long before he became US President, Lyndon B. Johnson was a head teacher at the Welhausen School in Cotulla, Texas, and later taught public speaking at both Pearsall High School and Sam Houston High. Billy Crystal was a junior high school teacher on Long Island, USA, while J.K. Rowling taught English in Portugal.

FAST FACT!

Other odd jobs famous people have had include lion tamer (actor Christopher Walken) and clown (actor Hugh Jackman).

The tin opener was invented decades after the tin can!

FAST FACT!
One of the earliest tin openers from 1865 featured a bull's head design.

Storing food in metal tin cans began in the Netherlands in the 18th century. The first large canning factories sprang up in Britain, France and the United States between 1813 and 1822, but tin openers didn't arrive until the 1850s. The first tin opener with a wheel to grip the edge of the tin arrived even later in 1870.

Before tin openers existed, people used whatever tools they could to puncture, chisel or cut through the metal tin.

One queen was so scared of fleas she had a tiny cannon built to fire cannonballs at them.

FAST FACT!

Queen Christina of Sweden succeeded the throne at the tender age of six. She later abdicated, and became leader of the art world in Rome, Italy.

Queen Christina was a Swedish monarch who was born in 1626 and died in 1689. She is said to have ordered the construction of the mini silver cannon (25.5 centimetres long) to fire tiny cannonballs at fleas in her bedroom.

She wasn't the only one with a dislike of creepy crawlies. English historian and politician Sir George Sitwell invented a tiny revolver so that he could shoot wasps in his garden.

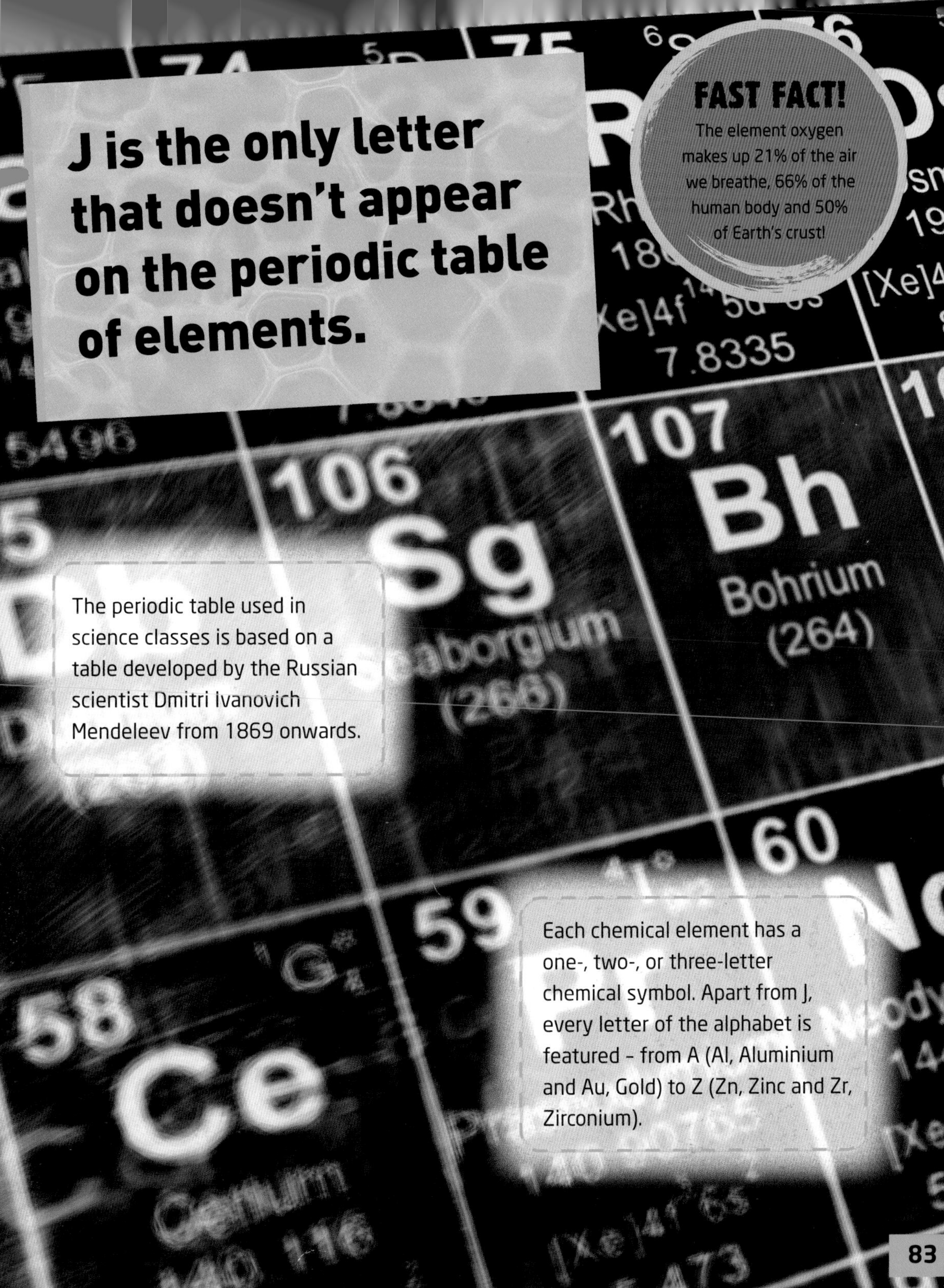

J is the only letter that doesn't appear on the periodic table of elements.

FAST FACT!
The element oxygen makes up 21% of the air we breathe, 66% of the human body and 50% of Earth's crust!

The periodic table used in science classes is based on a table developed by the Russian scientist Dmitri Ivanovich Mendeleev from 1869 onwards.

Each chemical element has a one-, two-, or three-letter chemical symbol. Apart from J, every letter of the alphabet is featured – from A (Al, Aluminium and Au, Gold) to Z (Zn, Zinc and Zr, Zirconium).

The volcanic eruption of Krakatoa in 1883 was heard 3000 miles away in Alice Springs, Australia.

Lying between the Indonesian islands of Java and Sumatra, Krakatoa's volcano erupted with enormous force. Dust and stones were sent as high as 56 kilometres up into the atmosphere, the island was ripped apart by the force and giant 30.5-metre high tsunami waves battered coastlines. The sound was heard across a large part of the world. People on Rodriguez Island in the Indian Ocean reported a sound like heavy gunfire, even though they were over 4600 kilometres away.

FAST FACT!

Fine ashes from the Krakatoa explosion made it all the way to New York City, USA!

The famous Dr Seuss book, *Green Eggs and Ham*, was written on a bet.

In the late 1950s, Theodor Seuss Geisel had just written his famous Dr Seuss book, *The Cat In The Hat*, using just 236 different words to help children learn to read. Then his publisher, Bennett Alfred Cerf, bet him that he couldn't write a successful children's book using even less words.

Geisel returned with *Green Eggs and Ham*, featuring only 50 different words. Both of these Dr Seuss books have sold over 7 million copies in the United States alone.

FAST FACT!

Dr Seuss was not a real doctor – he just added the title to his name for fun. His first book was rejected by 27 publishers.

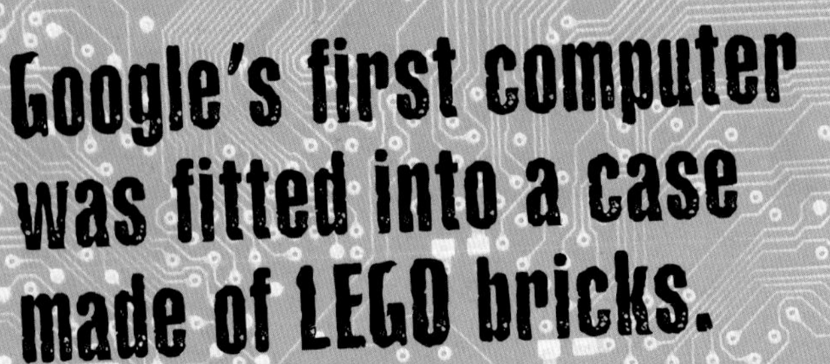

Google's first computer was fitted into a case made of LEGO bricks.

In 1996, Stanford University students Larry Page and Sergey Brin were building a computer to test their search engine program, called Pagerank, which became the core of the Google search engine.

FAST FACT!

In 2011, the Google company earned over £24 billion – more than enough to buy the LEGO group company many times over.

Having bought ten expensive hard disks to store all their data, Page and Brin needed a cheap case for their computer, so they built it out of LEGO bricks and plastic sheeting.

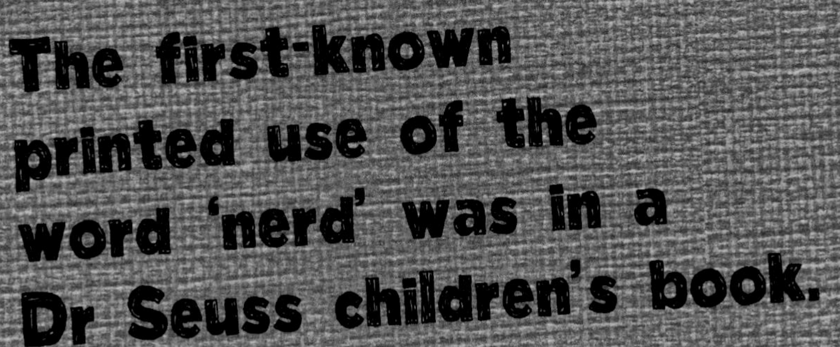

The first-known printed use of the word 'nerd' was in a Dr Seuss children's book.

A nerd is now a nickname for someone who is clever, often wears glasses, uses computers or studies hard and reads books intensely. But when it first appeared in Dr Seuss's 1950 children's book, *If I Ran the Zoo,* it was the name of an imaginary creature. From the 1960s onwards, the word became a popular way to describe a bookish person.

FAST FACT!

Dr Seuss's birthday, 2nd March, is now commemorated as National Read Across America Day.

In 1991, there was just one World Wide Web website. Today, there are more than 230 million.

The World Wide Web is used by hundreds of millions of people every day to learn, swap information, buy and sell goods and for entertainment. So, it's hard to get your head around how relatively new an invention it really is. British computer expert, Tim Berners-Lee, working at the CERN institute in Switzerland developed the first website, which went online at http://info.cern.ch in the summer of 1991.

FAST FACT!

Google estimated the Internet at about 5 million terabytes of data, which is 5 billion gigabytes or 5 trillion megabytes.

One aircraft pilot has been hijacked not once but twice during his career.

In 1931, the very first recorded plane hijacking occurred when Peruvian bandits hijacked a Ford Trimotor aircraft flown by American pilot Byron Rickards. In 1961, 30 years later, Rickards was piloting a Boeing 707 from El Paso, USA, when he was the subject of a second hijacking by two men who wanted the plane to fly to Cuba. Rickards and all onboard were rescued unharmed.

FAST FACT!

The world's first fatal hijacking happened in 1939, when Earnest P. 'Larry' Pletch shot his flight instructor Carl Bivens.

A newborn kangaroo is small enough to fit on a teaspoon.

Kangaroos give birth to really tiny babies which can weigh less than three grams. The newly born kangaroo lives in a special pouch called a marsupium on the mother's body for several months until large enough to enter the world on its own.

The largest species of kangaroo - the red kangaroo - can grow taller than an adult human and weigh more than 90.7 kilograms.

FAST FACT!

A red kangaroo can jump spectacularly far. An adult male red kangaroo can cover up to 7.6 metres in a single leap.

Grand Theft Auto IV was the most expensive computer game on its release, costing £67 million to make.

FAST FACT!

The game was so popular that it more than covered its costs in the first week of release, making over £334 million.

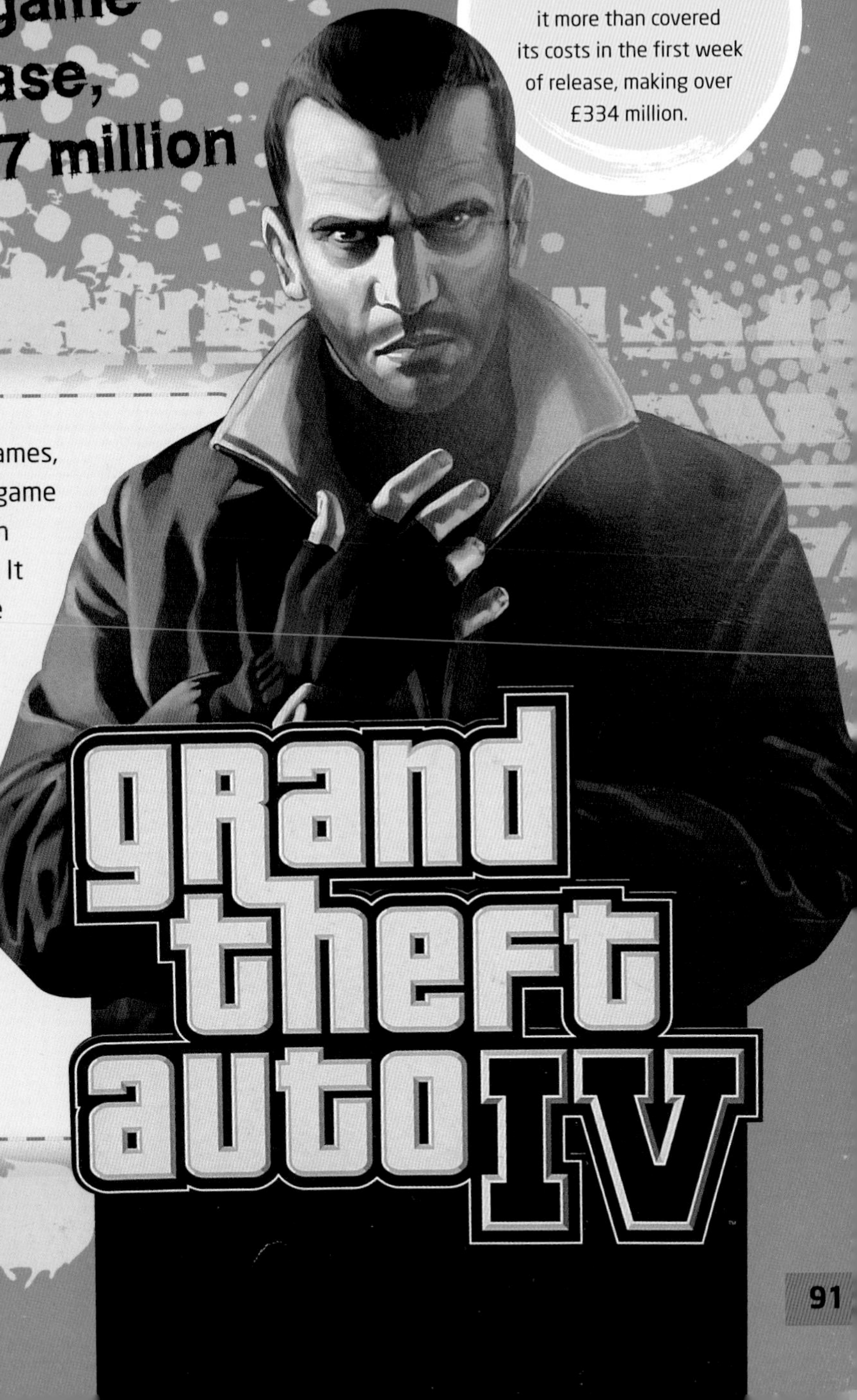

Created by Rockstar Games, this action-adventure game cost more to make than many Hollywood films. It took over 1000 people three-and-a-half years to produce the game, which includes many hours of music tracks and complex action scenes. Within three years of its 2008 release, the game sold more than 22 million copies.

grand theft auto IV

The Bombardier 415 fire-fighting aircraft can scoop up to 6100 litres of water in just 12 seconds.

FAST FACT!

The largest water bombing aircraft is a converted Boeing 747 airliner called the *Evergreen Supertanker*. It can hold 90,850 litres of water.

Firefighters tackling large forest and bush fires use water bombing aircraft that can skim a lake or the sea to scoop up large quantities of water. The aircraft then fly over the blaze and dump their load on the fire. The *Bombardier 415 Superscooper* has a wingspan of almost 28.5 metres and can take off and land from water or the ground. More than 70 of these aircraft have been built. They operate in the United States, Canada, France, Italy and Croatia.

A US nuclear power engineer working for NASA invented the Super Soaker toy water gun.

After a spell working at the Air Force Weapons Laboratory in the 1970s, Alabama-born Lonnie G. Johnson moved to California to work at NASA's Jet Propulsion Laboratory. There he helped to develop the nuclear power plant that was fitted to the *Galileo* space probe travelling to Jupiter. In 1989, when he was tinkering at home on designs for more powerful and fun water guns, he invented the first Super Soaker – now a best-selling brand of water guns that have sold millions.

FAST FACT!

The Super Soaker is just one of Johnson's 62 patents, ranging from hair-drying rollers to a wet-nappy detector.

More than 120,000 golf balls are lost every year on a single golf hole.

The killer hole is the 17th at the TPC-Sawgrass golf course in Ponte Vedra Beach, Florida, USA. It is short at around 120 metres from tee to the hole, but it features an island green surrounded by water. As a result, professional players and amateurs alike frequently see their ball land in the water. The course has to employ divers to recover many of the lost balls!

FAST FACT!

In the 17th century, golfers used feathery balls, which were made of boiled goose or duck feathers stuffed into a small leather pouch.

The dwarf planet Pluto was named by an 11-year-old schoolgirl.

FAST FACT!

It takes 248 Earth years for Pluto to complete an orbit around the Sun.

Some people think that the planet was named after the Disney animated dog, but it's actually the other way round. The planet got its name in 1930 when schoolgirl Venetia Burney from Oxford suggested the name *Pluto*, the Roman god of the underworld, to her grandfather when they were discussing the newly-discovered planet. He contacted his friend, astronomer Herbert Hall Turner. In less than two months *Pluto* became the official name of the planet.

An inventor made more than 5000 different prototypes of his invention before getting it right.

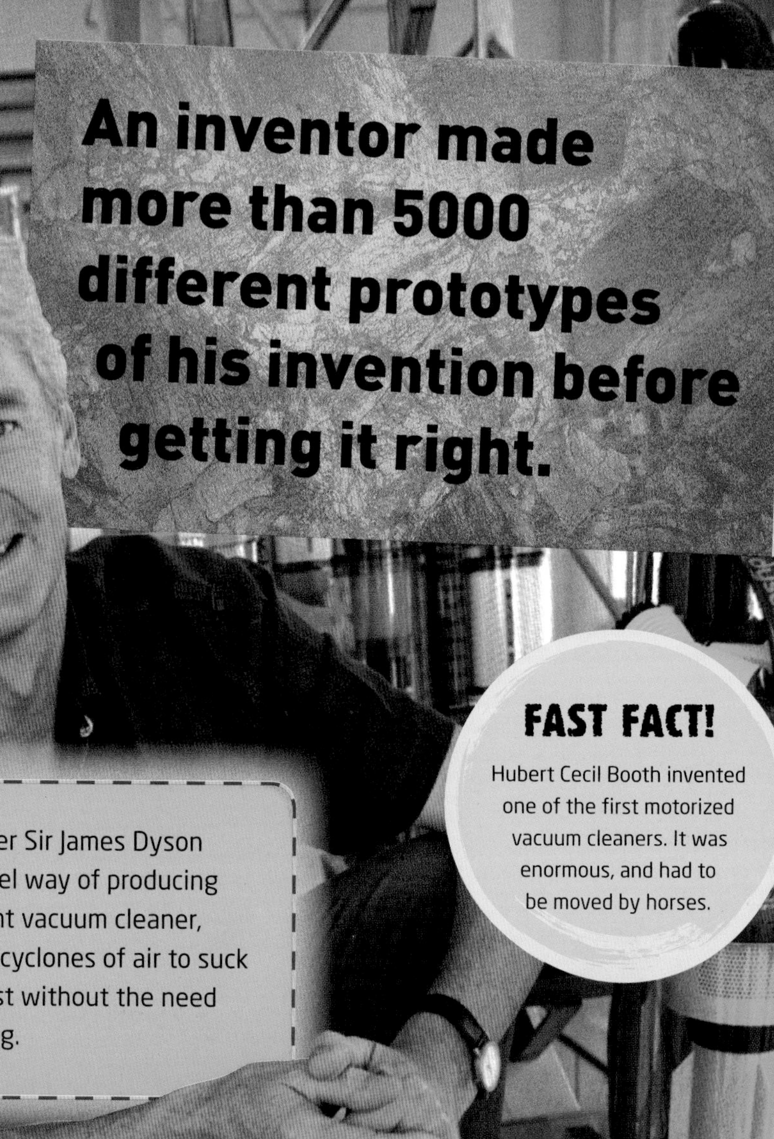

FAST FACT!

Hubert Cecil Booth invented one of the first motorized vacuum cleaners. It was enormous, and had to be moved by horses.

British engineer Sir James Dyson hit upon a novel way of producing a more efficient vacuum cleaner, using swirling cyclones of air to suck up dirt and dust without the need for a messy bag.

He had to make a staggering 5127 prototypes of the machine before his DC01 vacuum cleaner went on sale in the early 1990s. But Dyson now has a fortune of about £670 million as a result of his hard work.

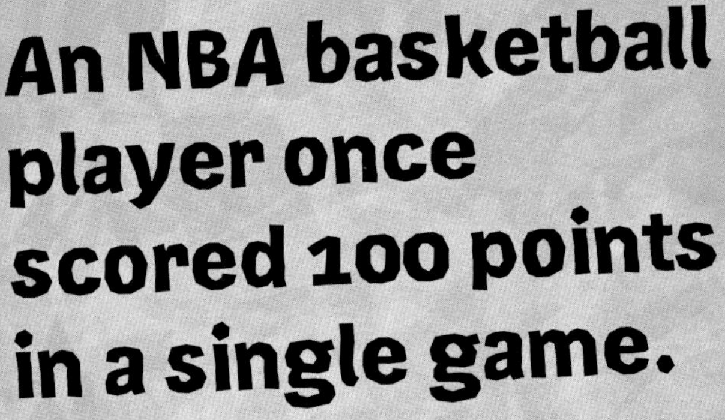

An NBA basketball player once scored 100 points in a single game.

That player was the great Wilt 'The Stilt' Chamberlain and he managed the feat playing for the Philadelphia Warriors against the New York Knicks in 1962. The 2.2-metre-tall American notched 23 points in the first quarter, 18 in the second, 28 in the third and up 31 points in the fourth, totalling 100 points in the 48-minute game. What makes it even more amazing is that it was in an era before players could score three points for a long-range basket – all of Wilt's points came from two-point shots or one point free throws.

FAST FACT!

In the 1961/62 season, Wilt Chamberlain scored an average of 50.4 points in each of the 80 games he played. Today, this record is thought to be unbreakable.

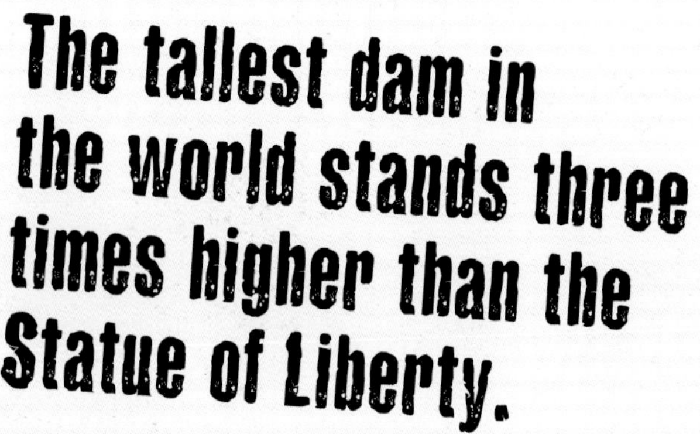

The tallest dam in the world stands three times higher than the Statue of Liberty.

FAST FACT!

The Kentucky Dam on the Tennessee River, USA, is 63 metres high and a whopping 2567 metres long. Now that is huge!

Dams are built to hold water for farming, to create a town water supply or to generate electricity at a hydro-electric power station. The oldest-known dam is in Jordan, and is about 5000 years old. The world's tallest dam – the Nurek Dam in the central Asian nation of Tajikistan – is much younger. It was completed in 1980 after 19 years of work, and measures 701 metres in length and 299 metres in height.

A monster truck once jumped over a Boeing 727 airliner.

FAST FACT!

The first monster truck was built in 1979 and called Bigfoot 1. A later model, Bigfoot 5, ran on 3-metre-high tyres, weighing 1089 kilograms each.

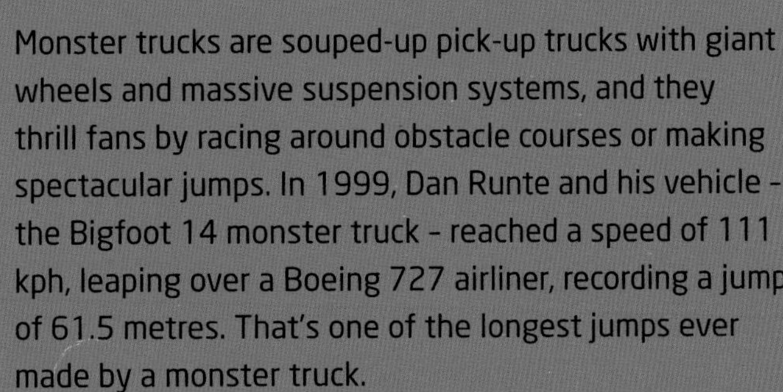

Monster trucks are souped-up pick-up trucks with giant wheels and massive suspension systems, and they thrill fans by racing around obstacle courses or making spectacular jumps. In 1999, Dan Runte and his vehicle - the Bigfoot 14 monster truck - reached a speed of 111 kph, leaping over a Boeing 727 airliner, recording a jump of 61.5 metres. That's one of the longest jumps ever made by a monster truck.

More rain fell in a day in Mumbai, India, than Chicago, USA, typically gets in a year.

You think of a heavy rain day when 2.5 centimetres of rain falls on your home town. The city of Chicago, USA, for example, averages about 86 centimetres of rainfall in an entire year. But on the 26th of July, 2005, a staggering 73.9 centimetres of rain fell in 24 hours in Mumbai. The resulting floods were devastating. The city's airports were shut down, thousands of lorries, buses and taxis were damaged or destroyed, and at least 5000 people died.

FAST FACT!

In contrast to the monsoon rains of Mumbai, parts of Chile are really, really dry. The average rainfall in the Antofagasta region is just 1 millimetre per year.

There are more robotic vacuum cleaners than any other type of robot in the world.

When you think of robots, you might think of space probes crawling around the surface of Mars, or robotic arms spray painting and welding cars in factories. But the most common robot on the planet is a small, disc-shaped, wheeled machine that navigates its own way around the house, vacuum cleaning the floors.

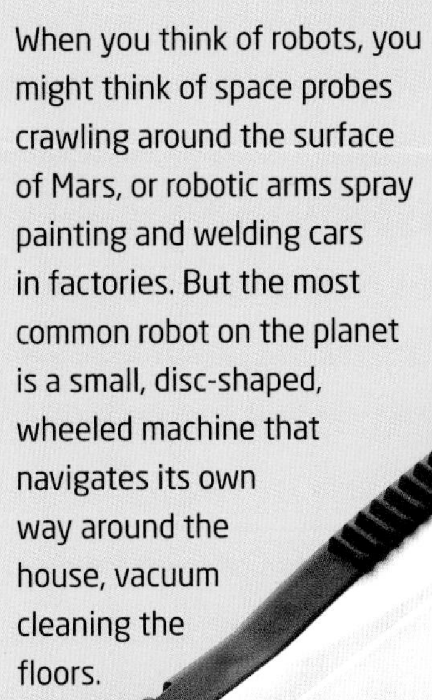

FAST FACT!

Roombas are so clever that they can sense the dirty areas in a room and spend a longer time cleaning them.

The first Roomba cleaning bot, built by iRobot, was launched in 2002. Since that time, more than 5 million Roombas have been sold, making it the world's most popular robot.

Bubblewrap was originally invented as wallpaper.

In 1957, Alfred W. Fielding and Marc Chavannes sealed two plastic shower curtains together, capturing air bubbles between them. Bubblewrap was born. The pair thought it would make funky wallpaper, but when it didn't sell well they offered it as insulation to keep heat inside greenhouses.

FAST FACT!

One extreme test - to show the power of bubblewrap - included wrapping up a pumpkin and dropping it from 10.6 metres. It survived without a scratch!

It was only when computer companies started to use bubblewrap to protect their hardware that sales of the material boomed. Now, enough bubblewrap is produced each year to circle Earth more than ten times.

An astronaut lost a £67,000 toolbag in space.

FAST FACT!

There are thousands of pieces of human-made debris orbiting Earth in space. The oldest one is the *Vanguard 1* space satellite, which launched in 1958.

NASA astronaut Heidemarie Stefanyshyn-Piper was a veteran of over 30 hours of spacewalks. But in 2009, while out in space repairing part of a solar panel powering the International Space Station, she had a major mishap.

A grease gun inside her toolbag had pumped grease all over the bag. As she tried to clean it up, the bag containing expensive tools floated away and out of reach. The toolbag orbited Earth for nine months before burning up in the planet's atmosphere.

A lion's roar can be heard up to 8 kilometres away.

FAST FACT!

A pride of lions can contain as many as 40 lions, though many prides are smaller.

These kings and queens of the African plains are one of only a handful of cats, including jaguars and leopards, which can produce a loud, deep roar – partly due to a special jointed bone in their throat called a hyoid. Of all the big cats, lions roar the most and the loudest.

An average male lion is 2.7 metres long, weighs around 160 kg and is very lazy. The males let the lionesses do more than three quarters of the hunting, and rest for up to 20 hours a day.

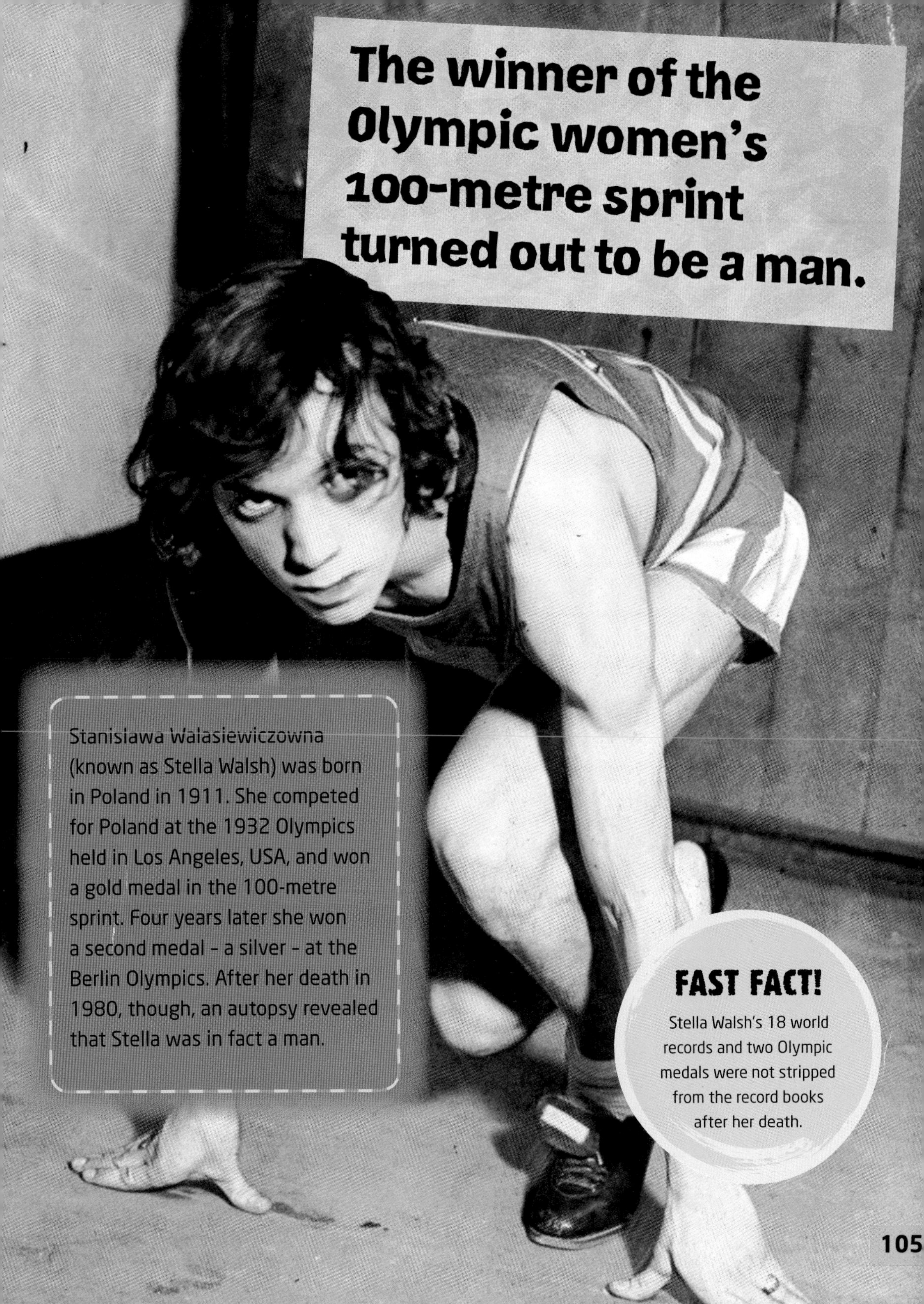

The winner of the Olympic women's 100-metre sprint turned out to be a man.

Stanislawa Walasiewiczowna (known as Stella Walsh) was born in Poland in 1911. She competed for Poland at the 1932 Olympics held in Los Angeles, USA, and won a gold medal in the 100-metre sprint. Four years later she won a second medal – a silver – at the Berlin Olympics. After her death in 1980, though, an autopsy revealed that Stella was in fact a man.

FAST FACT!

Stella Walsh's 18 world records and two Olympic medals were not stripped from the record books after her death.

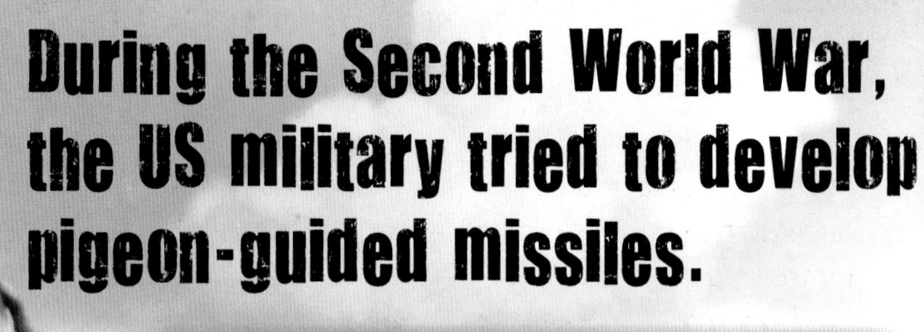

During the Second World War, the US military tried to develop pigeon-guided missiles.

American scientist B. F. Skinner received funding during the Second World War to build a missile control system. Pigeons were trained to tap on a screen showing the target whilst inside the missile.

FAST FACT!

Cher Ami was a First World War carrier pigeon that helped to save the lives of 200 trapped American troops by carrying a message about their location.

The missiles were never made, but pigeons were used in both the First and Second World Wars to ferry important messages. They were also used as experimental aerial photographers, carrying tiny automatic cameras to take pictures of the battlefields below.

A boxer knocked himself out.

Boxers often knock out their opponents, and occasionally even hit the referee. But in 1959, Henry Wallitsch sort of knocked himself out. While fighting Bartolo Soni at the Island Garden Arena in New York, USA, Wallitsch missed a punch, toppled out of the ring, and hit the floor hard. He was declared knocked out.

FAST FACT!

In June 1997, boxer Mike Tyson bit a chunk out of an opponent's ear during a fight. Tyson's boxing license was revoked and he was fined £1.9 million.

Picture Credits

Key: bg = background, m= main image, i = inset, t = top, b = bottom, l = left, r = right f = frame.

Almeda Country Fair: m p50,
Almay: p1bl Picturesbyrob, p19m Peter Horree, P32m Charles Polidano/ Touch The Skies, p48 bg Eye Ubiquitous, p54m Picturebyrob, 55m&i Dinodia Photos, p58i Royalty free images, p63m AlmayCelebrity, p64m Stephen Frink, p65m Adrian Sheratt, p69m AlamyCelebrity, p73m Robert Clayton, p107m GL Archive, p122m INTERFOTO, p127m North Wind Picture Archives, p135m Kathy de Witt, p146m America, p143mt Movie Store Collections, p143mb Medical-on-line, p170 Mim Friday, p172m DK, p182m RIA Novosti, p185m World History Archive, p187m Motoring
Picture Library, p188m Beepstock, p195m Paul Wood, p195i PJF News,
Corbis: p39m Bettman, p183m Michael Maloney/ San Francisco,
Dynamo: p1br Dan Cox, p7m Dan Cox,
FLPA: p20i Mitsuaki Iwago/Minden Pictures, p22m Donald M. Jones/ Minden Pictures, p38m Pete Oxford/Minden Pictures, p61 primrose Peacock, Holt, p77m Stephen Belcher/Minden Pictures, p83m Flip Nicklin/Minden Pictures, p83i Richard Herrmann/Minden Pictures, p94m Andrea Pistolesi, p97m Roland Birke, p99m Library of Congress/ digital version by Science Faction, p100i NBC/Contributor, p101m Topical Press Agency/Stringer, p115m Flip Nicklin/Minden Pictures, p125m Mark Raycroft/Minden
pictures, p171m Chris Newbert/Minden Pictures, P192m D P Wilson,
Getty Images: p5m Daniel Berehulak/Staff, p10m Gilbert Carrasquillo/ Contributer, p14m William James Warren, p15m Travel Ink, p16m Patrick McDermott/Contibutor, p17m Science Picture Co, p23m Keystone/
Stringer, p25m Bert Morgan/Contributor, p28m Antonio M. Rosario, p29i Jasper Juinen/Staff, p30i SuperStock, p33m Thomas Marent, p34m PhotoQuest/Contributor, p35m Hank Walker/Contributor, p37m Colin Anderson, p40m Gary Miller/Contributor, p41 Mark Dadswell/ Staff, P42m SuperStock, p45m Focus on Sport, p49m Scott Halleran, p52m Time Life pictures, p53m R.J. Eyerman, p56b Photosindia, p60m Silvestre Machado, p71b Ron Sachs, p76m Daniel Simon, p78m Michael Tran, p79m Datacraft Co Ltd, p86m Time Life Pictures/ Contributor, p87m Patty Wood/
Contributor, p89m Roy Stevens/Contributor, p98m Micheal Ochs Archives/Stringer, p92m Robert NICKELSBERG/Contributor, p102ml Mark Thompson/Staff, p108m Popperfoto/Contributor,p110m Photoservice Electra, p114m Thomas S. England/Contributor, p117m Michael M. Todaro/Contributor, p118i Dirck Halstead/Contributor, p128m Francis Miller, p157m David Maclain, p139m Sebastien Bourdon, p129m Rosie Greenway/staff, p147m Ben Stansell, p134m Barcroft Media, p145m Sonny Tumbelaka, p133m Photolibrary, p155m Toa Images Limited, p126m Flickr Open, p158m Paul Redmond, p140m Flickr Open, p131m Flickr, p132m Jeffrey Sylvester, p137m Dan Kitwood, p168m DEA Picture Library/ Contributor, p176m Huey Yoong, p182i Science & Society Picture Library/ contributor, p184m Jonathan Kitchen, p189m New York Daily News Archive/Contributor, p190m Melanie Stetson Freeman/ Contributor, p191m Chris Jackson/ Staff, p193bg STEVE GSCHMEISSNER,
NASA: p47m&I, p59m, p119i NASA/JPL-Caltech/Univeristy of Arizona, p82m, p91m, p91i NASA/Bill Ingalls, p96m, p150m, p165m, p173i,

Shutterstock: p1tl Leonello Calvetti, p1r Eric Isselee, p5b Lamella, p5i eldiv, p6b Triff, p6m James Thew, p6i zzoplanet, 8i Qoncept, p9bg Ssergey Kamshylin, p9m pandapaw, p11m Doug Lemke, p11i Ambient Ideas, p12it Georgios Kollidas, p12itf Anusorn P nachol, p12 im Africa Studio, p12ibgr Guzel, p12ibl Tatiana Popova, p13m Sebastian Kaulitzki, p17bg Sebastian Kaulitzki, p18m Georgi Roshkov, p18i valdis torms, p20b rehoboth foto, p20m Inc, p21b Sinisa Botas, p21m Petrafler, p24m VVK1,
p26m Jo Crebbin, p26i Andrew L., p27m kojihirano, p29b Madien, p30bgb James "BO" Insogna, p30mf Poprugin Aleksey, p30i leonello calvetti,
p31m DenisNata, p36m dezignor, p33bgb thewhiteview, p33 bgt Piotr Zajc, p39b Alhovik, p40b Cherkas, p40i Helena Esteb,
p42i Uryandnikov Sergey, p42bg jarvaman p43m Tami Freed, p44bg mathagraphics, p44i T-Design, p45i Marfot, p45bg Login, p46m Etienne du Preez, p47bg notkoo, p48i Michele Perbellini, p50bg Tamas Gerencser, p51m RimDream, p53bg Alice, p56bg ARENA Creative, p57m Tomasz Szymanski, p58i Peter Waters, p58i Julien Tromeur, p58bg Kuzmin Andrey, p59bg Irina Solatges, p60m Dan Thomas Brostrom, p62m
mmaxter, p62bg argus, p64m Antonio Abrignani, p64bg artcasta, p66i Jet Sky, p66bg alterfalter, p67m Ludmilla Yilmaz, p67bg Kororiz Yuriy, p68bg argus, p71bgt Login, p71bgb Irina Solatges, p71m Artsem Martysuik, p72m IDAL, p75m Alita Bobrov, p76bg Vladimir Nitkin, p78i Chichinkin, p78bg Ykh, p80m Zentilia, p85ir Globe Turner, LLC, p88m AlessandroZocc, p90m Anna Hoychuk, p84m Dudarev Mikhail, p85m newphotoservice, p85il
Alexander Zavadsky, p92i Rafal Cichawa, p93 m Photo Works, p95m Raywoo, p95i Leonello Calvetti, p100m thieury, p102bg Mario 7, p103m Herbert Kratky, p103bg Lukas Radavicius, p104bg pryzmat, p104m koya979, p105bg GlOck, p105m Eric Isselée, p106m John Kasawa, p109m Luciano Mortula, p111 Grzegorz Wolczyk, p112bg taweesak thiprod, p113m Neale Cousland, p115i Arno van Dulmen/ Shutterstock.com, p116m Markus Gann, p118bg edella, p120m Pal Teravagimov, p121m Michael Monahan, p121bg therealtakeone, p123 ArtTomCat, p124m Greg Perry, p129bg LongQuattro, p130bg Subbotina Anna, p130i Nikuwka, p136m Elena Schweitzer, p138bg Nilz, p138i Tovkach Oleg, p138i terekhov igor, p141m Nickolay Stanev, p142bg mitya73, p145m Martin Turzak, p148m Chris Fourie, p151m vectorgirl, p152m Byelikova Oksana, p153m rprongjai, p154m Richard Thorton, p156m Kim Reinick, p157i Le Do, p158bg Robert Adrian Hillman, p159m Eduard Kyslynskyy, p160m Volodymyr Krasyuk, p161m Senol Yaman, p161bg Laborant, p163bg Vector Mushrooms, p164m Dmitrijs Mishejevs, p166m Lefteris Papaulakis, P167 apiguide, p170bg Mario 7, p171i R-O-M-A, p173bg Triff, p173m BW Folsom, p174bg puruan, p174m NinaMalyna, p175m Eric Hui, p175i mary416, p176i Ilya D, Gridnev, p177m atribut, p176bg kentoh, p178bg Everett Collection, p178m Iouri Tcheka/ Shutterstock.com, p179m Anton Balazh, p179i Gillmar, p181m encikat, p186m RedTC, p186i Volker Rauch, p187bg fotomak, p188bg
Albachiaraa-, p192i Andy Fox Photography (UK), p193m Heidi Brand, p194bg -Albachiaraa-, p194m Ritu Manoj Jethani, p194i Ritu Manoj Jethani, p195bg PashOK, p196m Herbert Kratky, p196i Cathy Crawford, p197bg chris2766,
SPL: p119m US GEOLOGICAL SURVEY/ SCIENCE PHOTO LIBRARY